Inclusive Play

Inclusive Play

Practical Strategies for Children from Birth to Eight

Second Edition

Theresa Casey

Los Angeles | London | New Delhi
Singapore | Washington DC

SAGE Publications Ltd
1 Oliver's Yard
55 City Road
London EC1Y 1SP

SAGE Publications Inc.
2455 Teller Road
Thousand Oaks, California 91320

SAGE Publications India Pvt Ltd
B 1/I 1 Mohan Cooperative Industrial Area
Mathura Road
New Delhi 110 044

SAGE Publications Asia-Pacific Pte Ltd
33 Pekin Street #02-01
Far East Square
Singapore 048763

Library of Congress Control Number: 2009936572

British Library Cataloguing in Publication data

A catalogue record for this book is available from the British Library

ISBN 978-1-84920-123-0
ISBN 978-1-84920-124-7 (pbk)

Typeset by C&M Digitals (P) Ltd, Chennai, India
Printed in Great Britain CPI Antony Rowe, Chippenham, Wiltshire
Printed on paper from sustainable resources

372·21 0 CAS
000 23440

Dedicated to the memory of my Dad, John James Casey, and with love for my still radiant girl, Niamh

Praise for the first edition

'This book is an excellent resource, clearly written and methodical in its approach' (*Under 5*)

'The book was both enjoyable and thought-provoking, inspiring us as adults to develop our practice to remove barriers to inclusion and reflect on ourselves and the way in which we facilitate play for all children. It would be a useful tool for people new to the idea of developing inclusive play as well as encouraging experienced practitioners to reflect, question and continue to develop their inclusive play practice' (*Play Today*)

'As a practitioner, a trainer and a player I will want to keep this excellent publication close to hand, to offer to anyone working with children in the early years and beyond. I may well end up buying a second *Inclusive Play* book, one will not be on the shelf for very long! Play Development Workers with whom I work join me in saying that it looks good, you feel you want to pick it up and browse. All decided it is an excellent publication which they will use in a variety of ways and in a variety of settings. Certainly value for money!' (*Beppie Grace, Playmatters*)

Contents

About the author

Theresa Casey is an independent play consultant with special interests in inclusion, environments for play and children's rights.

Her career has spanned adventure play opportunities for children with disabilities and/or additional support needs in the UK, developing play projects for children in disadvantaged communities in Thailand, and supporting inclusion through play in schools and networks of community settings. She is known for the Play Inclusive (P.inc) Action Research project. Theresa is a Fellow of the Winston Churchill Memorial Trust and her work has been recognized through a number of awards. In 2008, Theresa was elected President of the International Play Association: Promoting the Child's Right to Play.

She keeps her hands dirty by spending a lot of time digging for worms and rounding up snails with her two young children.

Acknowledgements

This book is grounded in ideas emerging from the Play Inclusive (P.inc) Action Research project on which I worked with Susan McIntyre and colleagues from The Yard adventure playground in Edinburgh. P.inc itself was sparked by experiences in many different places; my thanks to the children, practitioners and parents whose inspired ideas I encountered along the way. Eilidh Blackwood gave us this lovely touchstone: 'Memories of having shared a really good time together are a resource on which to draw – a history of being happy together'.

Thanks for contributions of discussion, ideas and case studies from Ivan Harper, Harriet Blackmore, Fife Childcare playworkers, and many friends and colleagues in the International Play Association network around the world.

Thank you gorgeous children in the photos especially Jamie and Adam on the cover.

My continued thanks in this second edition to those who contributed wise words and photo opportunities to the first:

Margaret Westwood; Fiona Clark and Graeme Nicol then of Edinburgh Inclusive; Shirley Thomson and Louise Woodward then of the Play Action Team; Sandy Howe and Joyce Gilbert then of the Royal School of Dunkeld; Balgreen Nursery School, Edinburgh; Millbank Primary School, Nairn; St John's RC Primary School, Edinburgh; The Royal School of Dunkeld, The Yard, Edinburgh.

Thanks to Harriet for giving my children wonderful play opportunities while I neglected them to write and, as always, Jimmy Hewitt.

Introduction

I began the first edition of *Inclusive Play* by saying that 'somewhere in play is a conundrum. Play can be deeply serious or as light as air. It can be loud, abrasive, rude, smutty, hilarious, gentle or tender. It can fully absorb the whole attention of a child or of a group of children and yet can also be frivolous, throw-away or fleeting. It can be dangerous, dark and alarming. It can look like play and not be play, or vice versa'.

In revisiting *Inclusive Play* for the second edition, this conundrum continually floats in front of my eyes; every time I write down a suggestion or try to articulate a strategy, I find the opposite might also apply. For every possible scenario, several others present themselves – which is the beauty of working with children at play.

Inclusive Play is based on my experience of working with children of many different backgrounds, abilities, personalities and interests in adventure playgrounds, in settings in some very disadvantaged situations and in the day-to-day time spent playing with my own children. These experiences colour and inform what I do as much as the theory and ideas I have assimilated along the way. Sometimes it is very difficult to untangle these things. The result though I hope is strategies that are authentic and respectful of children, some of which will work for you and some to save for another day.

The second edition of *Inclusive Play* has been brought up to date in three particular ways as well as with a general refreshing. The current policy and guidance context which has moved on apace in the five years since the original *Inclusive Play* was written has all been updated, although I hope readers outside the UK will still find those mentions useful. It has been updated by upping the position of the play environment in the overall picture. An interesting and challenging physical environment is of such use to children and so helpful in supporting inclusiveness that it surprises me that we still fail to pay enough attention to it. Thirdly, *Inclusive Play* places children's play firmly within a children's rights perspective. Articulated in article 31 of the UN Convention on the Rights of the Child, the child's right to play can be understood as interrelated with all other aspects of the convention, rather than skipping along on its own. Play sits naturally with participation rights and the cultural rights with which it shares a stage, for example. When taken in this way, a very particular form of participation is suggested:

> Within the context of the whole convention, the right to play is the right to belong to a society which respects the approach of children as a very typical contribution to social life and to children's own development, even if this has characteristics (playfulness) that are unusual to adults. (van Gils, 2008)

This particular understanding of play has a different emphasis to that which would see play only as a vehicle for learning or a way to keep children out of trouble or a way to keep children fit and healthy, even if these are sometimes the welcome by-products of play.

A child rights approach offers challenges to current futuristic economic thinking in that it focuses on and organizes effort on the experiences of children in the here and now, and solicits their participation. Early intervention is not something that is done to young children in the hope of (re)shaping their future, but a collaborative venture with them. (European Commission, 2009: 47)

The concept of inclusive play links inseparably the right to play and the right of disabled children to participate fully in society. It embraces dimensions of richness, diversity and appreciation of difference. By aiming for inclusive play, we are simply aiming for the best play experiences we can offer to all children. We want play opportunities to be full of possibilities with which the children can engage and questions that they can pose for themselves.

Inclusive Play: Practical Strategies for Children from Birth to Eight in particular draws upon the findings of the Play Inclusive (P.inc) Action Research project. This project looked at the ways in which play supports inclusion of children with disabilities, first in schools and then in networks of community settings. An idea which continually inspired us in the project, drawn from the words of a particularly enlightened teacher, was 'Memories of having shared a really good time together are a resource on which to draw – a history of being happy together'.

This idea sits very well with the concept of play having intrinsic value beyond childhood and recognition of the human qualities of playfulness.

Play brings a raft of benefits in all areas of the children's being, well-being and development. Time spent playing is the natural arena for forming friendships, finding soul-mates and negotiating relationships. As well as these crucial social experiences, time spent at play is significant to how children view their whole experience of the settings they spend time in and for children with disabilities, to their whole experience of inclusion.

Aiming for inclusive play is crucial across the range of settings that children encounter in their early years. We may sometimes experience difficulty in marrying the desire to provide for truly free and spontaneous play opportunities within the constraints of our settings or professions. Sometimes pressure to achieve set goals can divert our attention away from how we achieve them, from the processes that children go through in creating for themselves meaningful, enriching and sustaining experiences.

The book addresses inclusive play in a way that aims to help practitioners apply the ideas and strategies flexibly in their own settings – whether Children's Centres, nurseries, out-of-school provision, schools or play schemes.

Terminology

Children

There are different views of the use of terms such as 'children with disabilities', 'disabled children' and 'children with additional support needs'. The phrase 'disabled children' is now preferred in some contexts. It reflects the concept that the child is disabled by barriers in society rather than by a particular impairment. There are many children and parents who do not like it, however, since it seems to emphasize 'disabled' over the child. The phrase 'children with additional support needs' reflects a broader sense of a requirement to respond to children's varied needs which may change over time. The phrase can encompass a broad spectrum: children who are experiencing difficulties or change, gifted children, refugees and asylum-seeking children, for example.

This book is about ways of ensuring that children are included in play and, through play, included in their setting. Therefore, in most cases, I have not found it necessary to describe children in terms of a particular impairment, need or circumstance. The reader should assume that when we talk about children, we are talking about children with a range of abilities, personalities, needs, backgrounds, talents and interests – and that these can change from day to day, if not from minute to minute!

Short descriptions and case studies of children at play in the book are 'composite' pictures drawn from different settings and experiences. They are intended to illustrate types of experience, interventions and processes. Names and details therefore do not identify any particular child or place.

Parents

Throughout this book, I have chosen to use the words 'parent' or 'parents' to mean the people who care for the child: mothers, fathers, foster carers or temporary care-givers, step-parents, grandparents, single parents, heterosexual or same-sex couples.

Teams

This book is for people working with children in a wide variety of settings. I have generally used the terms 'practitioners' or 'teams' to include people in the setting who can contribute to the experience of inclusive play. Inclusive play is more likely to take place within settings where inclusion is part of the ethos. Therefore, teams might include teachers, playworkers, specialist staff, volunteers, senior staff, janitors, nursery nurses, learning support staff, bus escorts, parents, visiting staff – the people who make up the community of the setting.

Facilitator

A number of activities are suggested throughout the text to enable teams to explore the ideas and suggestions proposed. Most would require one or two people to organize and facilitate the activity. The intention is that generally this person would be a practitioner from within the team although if you preferred you could ask someone external to help to facilitate to allow everyone to engage more fully.

Playtypes

The concept of 'playtypes' has become an increasingly familiar way of understanding the play of children we work with. Playwork theorist Bob Hughes
describes playtypes as 'the term we use to describe the different visible behaviours we observe when children are playing' (2006: xiii). Hughes proposed 16
playtypes, each subtly different from another and recognizable to an informed
observer. The concept of playtypes is enormously helpful in assessing the
opportunities available to children in our settings, in understanding the
choices they are making and to aid purposeful observation. References to playtypes are scattered throughout the text for this reason.

Quick actions for change

Sometimes making a relatively simple change can have an immediate effect,
benefiting both the children and the overall process of longer-term change.
You will find boxed 'actions for change' throughout the text. These are not
intended as alternatives to more profound changes to thinking and practice
but there are times when just getting on with it can be a good thing! A quick
action at the right time can sometimes be a catalyst for quite dramatic
progress, providing motivation and momentum for all involved.

1

Understanding inclusive play

The focus here is not solely on disabled children but on establishing an inclusive ethos to the benefit of everyone in the setting including staff, parents and members of the community of the setting. This chapter introduces some key ideas underpinning inclusive play, including:

- exploring children's play rights
- what we mean by inclusive play
- the value of inclusive play
- the particular benefits of good early years play experience for disabled children and those children 'on the margins'
- inclusive play and our youngest children
- making change: getting started
- a voice for children
- national play policies and strategies in the UK.

Exploring children's play rights

A first step to forming our strategies for supporting inclusive play is to bring a sharp focus back on to our understanding of play itself. By coupling the words 'inclusive' and 'play', we have created a phrase open to interpretation and some unpicking of what we are aiming for is vital. A definition of play has long been elusive; it's very ambiguity is a subject of study in itself (Sutton-Smith, 2001). Play's resistance to definition remains a challenge with which academics, policy-makers and practitioners grapple.

[handwritten margin note: definition of play.]

On top of that, most of us work in teams which bring together people from a number of professional and cultural backgrounds which, with our individual values and beliefs, have a bearing on how we 'read' and respond to children's play.

Since play was recognized in article 31 of the United Nations Convention on the Rights of the Child (UNCRC) in 1989, our thinking on play has taken on new dimensions; this required a shift to acknowledging that every child has a right to play from viewing play as at best a need but commonly as a frivolous way to pass time, a luxury not afforded by every child.

The UNCRC articulates the rights of children and the standards to which all governments must aspire. The Convention is the most universally accepted human rights instrument in history, ratified by the UK government in 1991 and at the time of writing by all but two countries in the world. By ratifying, governments have committed to protecting and promoting children's rights and have agreed to be held accountable for this commitment before the international community.

Article 31 of the United Nations Convention on the Rights of the Child

1. States Parties recognize the right of the child to rest and leisure, to engage in play and recreational activities appropriate to the age of the child and to participate freely in cultural life and the arts.

2. States Parties shall respect and promote the right of the child to participate fully in cultural and artistic life and shall encourage the provision of appropriate and equal opportunities for cultural, artistic, recreational and leisure activity.

Article 31 contains the apparently similar words rest, leisure, play and recreation. In their discussion of implementation, Hodgkin and Newell suggest that play is 'arguably the most interesting in terms of childhood, in that it includes activities of children which are not controlled by adults and which do not necessarily conform to any rules' (2007: 469).

This quickly takes us to the heart of the challenge; if play is not controlled or directed by adults, in which ways can we support play to happen without by our very involvement distorting it? This problem finds many echoes.

A government review in the UK took play to mean 'what children and young people do when they follow their own ideas, in their own way and for their own reasons' (DCMS, 2004: 9). This attempted to capture the concept of self-direction in play but has also been described as representing a 'significant field of tension' (Lester and Russell, 2008: 16). While on paper policy statements may project a central message that control of play should remain with the child, in practice the extent of support for enabling or even permitting the broad spectrum of playtypes and behaviours that might emerge when play is 'self-directed' is open to question.

Practitioners of necessity navigate these tensions while working with children on a day-to-day basis reconciling, if they can, the premise of play being controlled by children with requirements for planned or purposeful play and early learning goals. (Two examples with a slightly different emphasis, the first from England and the second from Northern Ireland, are given below.) Can we unravel planning for play and planning play, in a way with which we are content? There is no easy answer to this.

All the areas (of Learning and Development) must be delivered through planned, purposeful play, with a balance of adult-led and child-initiated activities. (DCSF, 2008a: 11)

Children should have opportunities to experience much of their learning through well-planned and challenging play. Self-initiated play helps children to understand and learn about themselves and their surroundings. (Interboard, 2006: 6)

As a starting point, it would be fair to say that the guidance within this book is aimed firmly at supporting play that is 'freely chosen, personally directed, intrinsically motivated behavior that actively engages the child' (NPFA, 2000: 6), a description of play widely accepted by play practitioners if open to criticism that there are, inevitably, exceptions to the rule.

By extension, the book is concerned with supporting children to reach the point where this is the way they are able to play if that is what they choose. For many children – including some disabled children – at least some of the time free play of this sort is unlikely to happen in a way that is satisfying to them without some additional support (direct or indirect) from peers or informed adults.

There is a strong link between article 31, the right to play, and article 23 of the UNCRC, the right of disabled children to 'enjoy a full and decent life, in conditions which ensure dignity, promote self-reliance and facilitate the child's active participation in the community' (UNICEF, 1989). The General Comment on the rights of disabled children issued by the UN makes this link explicit.

> The attainment of full inclusion of children with disabilities in the society is realized when children are given the opportunity, places, and time to play with each other (children with disabilities and no disabilities). (UNCRC, 2006: 19)

Play is so much a part of children's day-to-day lived experience that it represents at a very fundamental level the extent to which they participate in their communities. Restricted opportunities for play can be seen as a form of discrimination (UNCRC, 2006: 5). Concern was expressed in the 2008 report to the UK government (UNCRC, 2008: 12) that disabled children continue to face barriers to enjoyment of their rights, highlighting access to leisure and play as a current and ongoing issue.

In the UK, the Special Educational Needs and Disability Act 2001 amended the Disability Discrimination Act 1995 to make unjustified discrimination by education providers against disabled pupils, students and adult learners unlawful. The Disability Discrimination Act 2005 took things further, giving most public authorities a positive duty to promote disability equality. And going back to the UNCRC again, article 29 lays out the agreement undertaken by governments that education should be directed to 'the development of the child's personality, talents and mental and physical abilities to their fullest potential'.

At a practice level, putting rights into practice demands that we ask ourselves questions. What do we really mean when we say our settings are 'inclusive', that we are responding to 'the right to play' or the right to be included? What does it suggest about the direction of our practice and goals or the philosophy of the setting? Does it reflect the experience of the children who use the service or setting? Do they *feel* included?

The following short exercises can be used to explore what play and inclusion mean in our settings. They should involve as many different people as possible from the community of the setting and can be adapted to use with children as a way of exploring their experience of inclusion and play (suggestions are given below).

Activity

What we mean by inclusive play

'Inclusive play' is now a commonly used term but the meaning may be neither clear nor shared. This group activity aims to spark discussion and reflection. It is important that the facilitator of the activity sets a non-judgmental tone emphasizing that they are not looking for right or wrong answers, but rather some discussion of different points of view. The facilitator should be familiar with the thinking behind medical and social models of disability and about integration and inclusion. Information is given below which could also be used in handouts to support this activity. The discussion can be set up in one group – up to perhaps a dozen if people feel comfortable with that – or smaller groups of three or four.

- Copy the 'Discussion starters' below, or create your own (suggestions below) and cut into separate slips of paper. You may prefer to remove the sources so that these don't influence the direction of discussion.
- Lay these slips face down. A member of the group should pick one at random and read it out. One member of the group can be designated as the reader if that is more appropriate to the group.
- This person begins the discussion by sharing any thoughts or questions it brings to mind and other members of the group are encouraged to join in the discussion.
- Use as many or as few of the discussion starters as seems appropriate.
- One person could be designated as a recorder to note common themes or key phrases and questions on large sheets of paper as they arise.

Discussion starters

- Memories of having a really good time together are a resource on which to draw – a history of being happy together.
- For inclusion to work, children should get one-to-one support to prepare and support them into mainstream. They do need lots of help and preparation first.
- I just want to be with who I want to be with, hanging out really.
- Inclusive play means enabling each child to play and express themselves in their own way and supporting them to play together when they wish to.
- I know that inclusion will probably never happen as everything gravitates towards what's normal and what's acceptable and what we can all relate to. People like to pigeon-hole other people and if they are different, they think 'oh, they don't fit in'.
- Disabled children are not just the responsibility of specialist disability services. All services need to ensure that disabled children can take part in everything they do. (The Inclusion Charter – source online: www.edcm. org.uk/inclusioncharter)
- Inclusion means a deep commitment and awareness that there is a very wide range of human behaviour and understanding of the world; that there is a respect for different perceptions of life.
- In a school setting, inclusion can mean that the total environment has meaning and is accessible to everybody: that it is safe; that it is clear what everything is for; that it is functional.

- If the children are all just absorbed in their own thing, I don't think that is inclusion.
- True equality of opportunity is about making sure that everyone has the power to help shape the society they live in. (Source online: www.equalityhumanrights.com)

Note: all discussion starters without accompanying sources originate from the Play Inclusive (P.inc) Action Research Project.

Further discussion starters specific to your setting can easily be created:

- look for definitions of inclusion and inclusive play in your own or other organizations' policy and guideline documents, in statements from disability, play or children's rights organizations, or on the Internet
- ask children, parents and colleagues for their definitions. Try using a dictaphone to quickly capture some views. This is a nice way to adapt the activity for children
- gather visual discussion starters such as photographs, pictures from newspapers or video clips.

Further discussion points

- Does the discussion suggest a common understanding or definition of 'inclusive play' within the group?
- How does this compare with the practice in your setting?

Medical and social models of disability

The medical and social models of disability reflect two ways in which disability is understood. They influence how people react to, think about and act towards disabled children and adults.

The medical model views disabled children as having an illness or problem that needs to be cured. This illness or problem is a hurdle which they need to get over in order to take part in 'normal' society. They require help from experts who are in the best position to determine what will be the most suitable treatment for them. If they cannot be cured, then they should be cared for. This attitude is very pervasive in many societies and lots of us have unconsciously absorbed aspects of it.

The social model of disability was developed by disabled people as a challenge to the medical model. The social model recognizes that some people are disabled by barriers in society that exclude and discriminate against them, for example through attitudes that favour non-disabled children and adults, through physical barriers and in the way we organize things. Let's have a look at a few examples of each of these from children's settings.

- the assumption that all disabled children will require one-to-one assistance, thereby allowing children to be excluded on the basis of not being able to afford enough staff

- having equipment stored in cupboards with written labels only, with the consequence that some children are prevented from making independent choices because they do not know what equipment is stored where

- entrance criteria which insist that only children from the local school can attend the provision, thereby excluding children who attend special schools or units.

Removing these attitudinal, environmental and organizational barriers is a priority within the social model. It is also the approach taken in this book.

Integration or inclusion?

The terms 'integration' and 'inclusion' are sometimes used interchangeably and often very loosely. Integration tends to suggest that disabled children can be part of a children's setting if they are able to adapt to it. This places the emphasis on ensuring the child is equipped with particular skills or has achieved particular standards so that he or she is able to fit in.

Inclusion has a broader meaning, placing the onus on our settings to ensure that we are open and prepared to welcome children with a range of abilities, backgrounds and personalities as a matter of course; that we respect the right of the child to be there and expect to provide a high quality experience for all.

The move from a concept of 'integration' towards 'inclusion' reflects a progression in the thinking about the rights of disabled children in society and about the roles of settings and institutions such as schools.

 Quick actions for change

- Obtain a copy of the United Nations *Convention on the Rights of the Child* and look for the rights relevant to play and inclusion. Look out for child-friendly versions to stick up on the walls.
- Graffiti children's rights as slogans around your setting.
- Dedicate some shelf space to inclusive play resources in your staffroom, office or parents' meeting room.

 Activity

The value of inclusive play

Playing allows children to develop a sense of well-being, develops their emotional responses, and improves their interpersonal skills. It involves exploration and creativity, helping children think in a flexible manner, developing the creative process, language skills, and learning and problem solving skills. Playing in natural spaces is particularly beneficial as these are open to more opportunities for play. (DCSF and DCMS, 2008: 10)

Play of course has crucial and wide-ranging benefits to children and the people around them, both benefits in the here and now and those that they will carry with them into the future. Taking as a starting point that children do need to play and benefit from it, this activity looks in particular at the benefits of 'inclusive play' and what is gained through shared experiences of play, perhaps with some support.

Using Figure 1.1 as an example, on a very large sheet of paper, draw out rippling concentric ovals with the headings: Children, The Setting, The Community of the Setting and Wider Society. Don't add in the rest of the text.

- The facilitator asks colleagues to write down all the benefits of inclusive play they can think of on sticky 'post-it' notes.
- Each idea goes on a separate note.
- Each person sticks up their notes onto the appropriate space within the concentric ovals.
- Similar and related benefits are then grouped together and headings are created for these.
- This provides a rich picture. The group looks for any gaps, contradictions or discussion points.
- The facilitator helps to review and sum up the activity.

Following the discussion, you can use the material by sticking it all down firmly or making it into a poster and displaying it in a public area to prompt more discussion.

The particular benefits of good early years play experience for disabled children and those children 'on the margins'

When considering inclusive play, we often start by thinking about children who are identified as needing help because of an impairment or additional support need. However, when looking at and then developing our provision for play, it's often noticeable that there are children who flit around on the margins and are rarely engaged in play or play with others. These children often gain enormously from changes within the environment or sensitive support. The message from inclusive play is that it makes it better for everyone.

Play is crucial to children's experience of a setting (settings in which play is the primary objective or one way of working). Whether or not the staff are pleasant, the buildings adequate, the programme varied, if the time spent at play with peers is unsatisfactory then that can set the tone for the child's whole view of the setting. The work of hospital play specialists illustrates this well; good medical treatment isn't enough for children to feel positive about their spells in hospital and children's opportunities for play will aid their adjustment, coping and recovery.

Child-mediated play (particularly outdoor play, school playtime, free play with low levels of adult intervention) is especially important to how included children feel. These are the opportunities for children to have a place among peers and take part in the particular culture of play in that place. Children's play culture can have its own language, fads and phases, values, even its own history and geography as seen in the play landscapes children create and recreate for themselves.

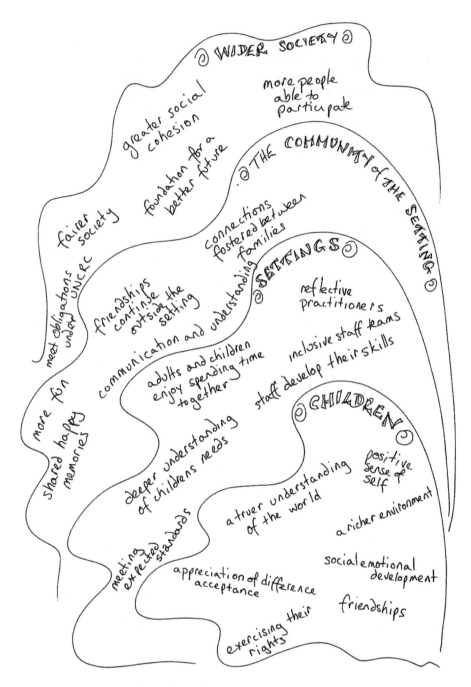

Figure 1.1   The benefits of inclusive play

Acceptance by peers is significant in the development of a child's sense of self and personal identity. We can all remember from our own childhoods how quickly children see through well-intentioned social engineering by adults so child-mediated play is particularly important. In play, children may have to 'take on the world' and learn about relationships, how they work and are negotiated including through teasing, falling out, making up, loyalty, quarrels, shifts in groups, jealousy and so on. These are real experiences that all children have to tackle and learn about.

When discussing inclusion with children, friendship is usually at the centre. Friendships developed through specific attempts to provide for inclusive play can be carried over into other parts of their lives. A friendship developed at playtime or in a playscheme has the possibility of developing into play in the children's local community or homes. These are the types of experiences that are stifled before they even have a chance to develop, when children are not able to access local play provision.

Play provokes wide-ranging language and communication and through inclusive play, children will hear flexible use of language by peers including slang, word play and hilarious rude words. There is enormous motivation to use language in play and flexible use of non-verbal communication can often be more readily exchanged in the context of play. Play also offers opportunities for behaviour and traits to be appreciated in a way they might not be elsewhere – taking daring risks, making rude noises, mimicry, silliness, jokes or telling unbelievable tales.

Many children with disabilities have few areas in their lives in which they feel able to exercise real choice and control. It may be because of change or disruption in their lives, because they spend a great deal of time having treatments or therapy, or simply because they have to rely on adults to get them around. Play can be a process through which they can regain a sense of control or work through difficult or challenging experiences. Play environments which have elements that can be manipulated, and that can cope with processes of creation and destruction, are of great importance to children. (See Chapter 2 for more on play environments.)

Risk and challenge are integral parts of the play experience and it has been said that children with disabilities have an equal if not greater need for opportunities to take risks, since they may be denied the freedom of choice enjoyed by their non-disabled peers (Play Safety Forum, 2002). Children need opportunities in their play to learn to judge their own capacities and extend them, explore limits and to experience excitement, nervousness, courage, daring, thrills and real spills. (Chapter 5 looks at this in more detail.)

Ultimately, it is in the nature of play that there is no right or wrong. It is therefore an arena in which children with additional support needs can be themselves, making their own meaning, gaining their own satisfaction from play in their own way and at their own pace.

This presents a particular challenge to adults who find it very difficult to gauge the level and type of support to provide without intruding and therefore disrupting the very dynamic they hope to support. It is this particular challenge that is a central issue in providing for inclusive play and we look at it in more detail in Chapter 3.

Inclusive play and our youngest children

Inclusion starts early. From the very earliest age, disabled children should have the right to play and learn with other children, enjoying all aspects of life and friendship that other children do. (The Inclusion Charter – source online: www.edcm.org.uk/inclusioncharter)

Finally, in this section, a mention of rights and our youngest children. The early years are a period of amazing growth and change with mobility, communication and understanding developing rapidly. Children are building relationships and emotional attachments and interests and abilities are emerging. Early childhood is also a critical period for realizing children's rights. In 2005, the UN children's committee issued a General Comment on implementing child rights in early childhood with objectives including to encourage recognition of young children as social actors from the beginning of life, with particular interests, capacities and vulnerabilities, and of requirements for protection, guidance and support in the exercise of their rights (UNCRC, 2005: 2).

> Babies and infants are entirely dependent on others, but they are not passive recipients of care, direction and guidance. They are active social agents, who seek protection, nurturance and understanding from parents or other caregivers, which they require for their survival, growth and well-being. (UNCRC, 2005: 8)

In our work with children, beginning with a perspective of young children as 'active social agents' helps to inform practice and the experiences we make available, with a view to responding to children as they are now. Their need to do what their one-, two- or three-year-old self needs to do rather than preparing them for what they might need to do later, is paramount.

Making change: getting started

All teams need to invigorate and refresh their ideas from time to time: the dynamics of play change with different groups of children, adults, seasons, and spaces and places to play. Practitioners with distinct professional roles may want to consider the benefits to be gained within their area of concern and therefore how they see their role, with others, in providing for or supporting inclusive play.

The following quick exercises are always useful:

- Swap roles: a teacher could take the place of a playground supervisor for the day; a playworker from the after school club could come into the nursery class; an occupational therapist could make playground observations. It is easy to fall into set expectations of children and ourselves. Swapping roles can give insight into children's needs, abilities and personalities in a different environment, allowing them to surprise us.

- Make a change in the environment and watch what happens. Are new possibilities opened up? Does it influence patterns of play or groupings of children? There are numerous ways to do this quickly:

  - Throw a tarpaulin over the branch of a tree.
  - Introduce music: hide a CD player in some bushes and play intriguing music from it; ask some music students to set up in a corner of the play space and play classical music during the play session; set out some sturdy percussion instruments.
  - Hang billows of ribbon from a doorframe.

- Make a trail around the play space with chalk, stones or shiny paper.
- Make a cave with tables and dark cloths.
- Leave out a pile of big cardboard boxes.

- Observe: spend a bit of time quietly in the play space observing the children at play as unobtrusively as possible. You could look out for different types of play, groupings of children, interactions, preferred places, preferred play materials, use of the whole space.

- Check out your observations with the children at an appropriate moment that doesn't disrupt their play. Make it positive: 'I noticed you all doing something really interesting when you were in that corner ... can you tell me about it?' Children are often really keen to talk about their play provided you are genuinely interested and listening, and not seeking to intervene, direct or judge.

- Encourage other members of the team to observe play at the same or different times. Compare your observations. It is interesting how differently adults can interpret the same play situation having seen it from different angles or with different levels of involvement.

- Recognize that you cannot be invisible in a play space and that you may find children are curious to find out what you are up to. One useful strategy is to involve them in what you are doing. Ask them to go off and survey their friends for you on what they are doing. A little notepad and pencil in their pocket will give them a role.

 Case study

We are very aware of the importance of the outdoors in a child's development and therefore our outdoor space is an integral part of our nursery. We have a small, enclosed nursery garden which we developed with the help of parents, creating an area we felt was rich in learning and experiences.

We were upset when we were unable to access our play area due to building work in the school. For a two-week period, we took our children up to the primary school field to play instead. The children loved the big open space where they could run freely, play with balls and hide and seek. It was a great opportunity for us to observe children's play in a way we cannot do in the confines of our nursery garden. For example, we picked up on one child's difficulty in running which enabled us to focus further on his development and how we can best support him; we could see that some children had little experience of being in a wider space from their initial lack of confidence and ideas about how to play out there; some children were very competent at using whatever they found – twigs and grasses etc to play with; the school's play apparatus posed a bigger physical challenge in comparison with the nursery garden and it was great to see the children's perseverance.

As a result of our observations, we now aim to take the children to the big field more frequently in future.

A voice for children

Listening to and engaging with children, acting on their recommendations, following up on the views that children have expressed through behaviour, actions and words are important in all children's settings. These processes, anchored in the children's day-to-day experiences, form the basis of an ongoing dialogue.

A culture of participation is important to the development of inclusive play. Inclusion is an ongoing process, and in inclusive play we need to be sure we are continually acting on our observations and responding to individual needs within groupings of children.

Each child's experience is unique. For children with disabilities or additional support needs, their perception of the world and experience of it may not be like our own and we cannot act on assumptions or on assumed models of ages and stages.

> The Convention (on the Rights of the Child) envisages a change in relationship between adults and children. Parents, teachers, caregivers and others interacting with children are seen no longer as mere providers, protectors or advocates, but also as negotiators and facilitators. Adults are therefore expected to create spaces and promote processes designed to enable and empower children to express views, to be consulted and to influence decisions. (UNICEF, 1989)

Figure 1.2 illustrates some of the Why? Who? When? Where? How? and What? of encouraging participation.

Use Figure 1.2 as the basis for a 'mind map'; take the whole figure or redraw it as separate circles on separate sheets of large paper. Ask colleagues to elaborate on the points in each circle, adding for example discussion and action points, barriers or opportunities.

There are many ways to find out more about children's own experience of play and play environments. Quiet observation of children's play (informed by knowledge of the children themselves, of play and of children's needs) is one of the most fundamental. Other suggestions include:

- Chatting to the children and asking about their likes, dislikes and preferences. Informal chatting is often very fruitful and shouldn't be overlooked as a method of consultation.

- Actively building up the children's experience of expressing themselves through creative opportunities in the setting. Always have art materials freely available for the children to use. Visit galleries, exhibitions, theatres, watch street theatre, hold workshops, stage mini-performances – all of these will help the children to build up their language of expression.

- Encouraging the children to interview each other about their views. Using a dictaphone lends an air of authenticity to being a 'reporter' and means the child doesn't have to be able to write replies down. A schedule of questions can be drawn up with visual prompts as well as text.

- Spending time with children in their special place or doing something they really enjoy allows you to explore their preferences more deeply and shows them you really are interested in the things they like to do. For example, you

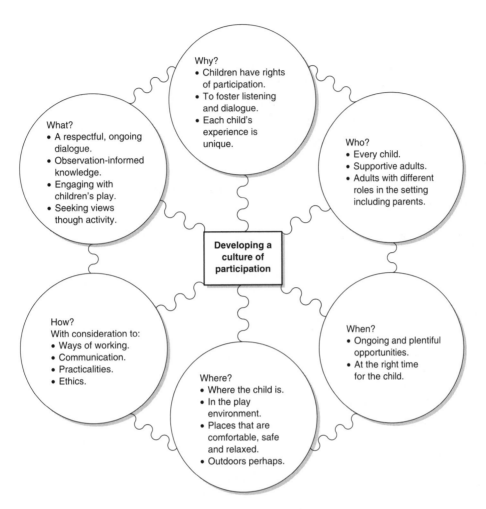

Figure 1.2   A culture of participation supports inclusive play

could sit quietly with a child (if they allow) in a spot they enjoy and share in the sensory experiences that the child gains (the sound of the wind, the flickering of light through moving leaves, the sensation of being in a little enclosed space, for example). The children might share with you otherwise overlooked details that make the space special to them, such as a hollow in a branch or a gap in a hedge to peek through.

- Creating the story of playtime: what playtime is like for me. Ask children for their play and play experiences as though they were telling a story: 'I went out to play and …'

National play policies and strategies in the UK

In 2002, the Welsh Assembly Government published its play policy. The *Play Policy* and *Play Policy Implementation Plan* (2006) are available from the Welsh Assembly Government (see http://wales.gov.uk/topics/educationandskills/publications).

(Continued)

(Continued)

The Welsh Assembly Government believes that: play is the elemental learning process by which humankind has developed. Children exhibit a behavioural imperative and instinctive desire to play. It has contributed significantly to the evolutionary and developmental survival of our species. Children use play in the natural environment to learn of the world they inhabit with others. It is the very process of learning and growth, and as such all that is learnt through it is of benefit to the child. (WAG, 2006: 2)

The English *Play Strategy* was published in 2008 as a 'commitment from the Children's Plan' (and is available from www.teachernet.gov.uk/publications):

Our vision for 2020

1.1 The Play Strategy is key to achieving our ambition to make this the best place in the world for children and young people to grow up. Play is a vital ingredient of a happy and healthy childhood. (DCSF, 2008b: 11)

The Play and Leisure Policy Statement for Northern Ireland was published in 2009 by the Office of the First Minister and the Deputy First Minister (OFMDFM) (and is available from www.allchildrenni.gov.uk/index/play-and-leisure-policy.htm):

The vision for play is: to recognise, respect and resource play is to recognise, respect and value childhood. (p. 3)

The aim of the policy is to establish play within a policy framework that will place high value on play and leisure as an essential element in the development of children's lives, families, communities and society.

(At the time of writing, Scotland does not have a national play policy or strategy – see Play Scotland for the latest information at www.playscotland.org)

☐ Summary

Once inclusive play starts to happen and people experience it working (even in small steps), it gathers momentum.

Being left out of play is one of the first signs of a child having difficulty. Children can become increasingly isolated over time despite other attempts to include them. When play is seen as a central way in which we ensure all children feel a valued part of the setting (since it is so important to them), then it supports the feeling of connectedness.

The ethos (the disposition or character) of a setting gains much from inclusive play. Most importantly, shared experiences which are authentic, memorable and happy contribute to a shared identity which each member of the community of the setting takes with them.

- It is important to spend time as teams exploring what we mean by inclusive play and how that relates to the practice in our settings.

- The model of inclusive play is informed by a number of things: the UN Convention on the Rights of the Child, the application of laws and our personal and professional values and principles.

- An approach informed by these allows us to start to reflect on whether the children in our settings are getting as much out of their play as they might – enjoyment as well as development – and whether all the children are really included.

- Children's experience both of inclusion and of play are unique and each child holds considerable knowledge and a range of experience.

- Participation and inclusion cannot be separated – inclusion is absolutely integral to any attempt to foster participative cultures based on children's rights.

- The benefits of inclusive play are wide-ranging and long-lasting, both in different and in common ways among members of the community of the setting.

Further reading

Else, P. (2009) *The Value of Play*. London: Continuum.

Lancaster, Y.P. (2003) *Promoting Listening to Children: The Reader*. Berkshire: Open University Press.

NPFA (National Playing Fields Association) (2000) *Best Play: What Play Provision Should do for Children*. London: NPFA/Children's Play Council/PLAYLINK.

2

Play environments that support, intrigue, challenge and inspire

This chapter works through strategies for creating play environments more supportive of inclusive play and considers:

- working with the play environment
- the influence of the environment on inclusive play
- the qualities of an inclusive environment
- playful environments for very young children
- assessing the environment for the opportunities it affords
- a locus for children's participation
- a play environment development plan.

Working with the play environment

The physical environment available to children is enormously important in supporting their play. It provides the tools and raw materials, the props and backdrops. The basic ingredients never seem to change: sand, water, earth, fire, changing weather and natural cycles, 'loose parts' to play with and people to interact with. Children need challenge in their play. They need support sometimes but they need to make mistakes and have accidents. Children need direct contact with the environment and with each other. They need first-hand experience: guddling in water, splashing through mud, squinting through sunlight, rolling in grass, digging in earth. After all, what is the point of providing services for young children, if they can't then play in the dirt or dig up worms, fall out of a tree, climb on a branch or a boulder, build a dam, fly a kite, get wet, get dirty, get tired, get bored even?

The physical environment can support children to take hold of and witness the processes of change, creation and destruction. It provides adults with the opportunity to observe and document (to help to make the processes visible). Although indoor spaces are very important to play, outdoor environments almost always appear the place of choice for children's play.

The play environment (a school playground, field, patch of overlooked garden, adventure playground – whatever you have access to) can provide a platform which allows the children's own interests, preferences and play skills to come to the fore. Interactions between children often develop more naturally when they are intrigued by something another child is doing or drawn to a focal point which has sparked mutual interest.

 Case study

A pink tarpaulin tent provided a focal point for interaction. Gary and Hamish particularly enjoyed its sensory properties, running underneath it, through the pink glow, the fabric rustling and floating around them. The game developed, with one following the other like a shadow, under the tent and around the back to go under again, occasionally laughing or glancing at each other.

Staff commented that these children don't usually get along and never play together.

(*Source*: McIntyre, 2007: 24)

A successful play space is a place in its own right, specially designed for its location, in such a way as to provide as much play value as possible. (Shackell et al., 2008: 16)

A number of sets of principles and guidelines can be applied to settings aiming to provide for play (with new designs or upgrades of existing provision). These can help you think through what you have got and what you would like to aim for. The specifics of such guidance vary. For example, the areas to consider suggested by Stirling Council's design guide (Gutteridge et al., 2007) are useful and can be summarized as:

- space (dealing with negotiating adequate space and creative solutions for shared space) and boundaries (to create a secure space)

- access (including maximum integration between indoors and out), storage (for outdoor equipment) and surfaces (gravel, grass, bark, etc., preferable to 'safety surfaces')

- levels (with a change of height and perspective)

- sand (as a surface and 'working' area)

- water (provided by puddles, outside taps or various water features)

- planting (to fulfil many purposes)

- shade and shelter (for all weathers)

- seating and perches (story circles to boulders and fallen tree trunks, etc.)

- supervision, care and autonomy (balancing need, privacy and autonomy with supervision).

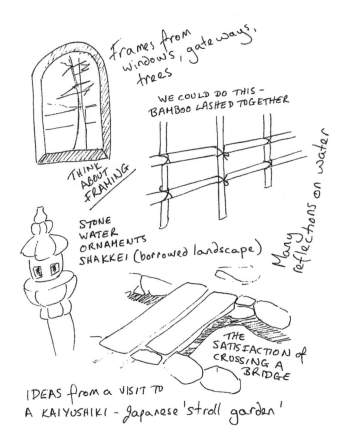

Figure 2.1 Ideas collected from a field visit

Recent government guidance (Shackell et al., 2008: 16–21) used a formula of ten principles asking the reader to 'imagine a play space': designed to enhance its setting; in the best possible place; close to nature; where children can play in different ways; where disabled and non-disabled children play together; loved by the community; where children of all ages play together; where children can stretch and challenge themselves in every way; maintained for play value and environmental sustainability; that evolves as the children grow.

Have a think through what is being suggested and then identify the considerations which are most important to your setting. Use them in conjunction with visits to a range of spaces children enjoy playing in and make sure you look at it all with a 'critical eye' – that is don't assume that children will prefer the spaces or equipment that have been specifically provided for play over informal, natural or overlooked play spaces (beaches, cemeteries, back yards, formal gardens, etc. – see Figure 2.1).

Structural, semi-permanent, temporary and ephemeral features

You might also find it useful to think of the play environment in layers which have varying life spans, allowing the space to remain flexible, responsive and stimulating.

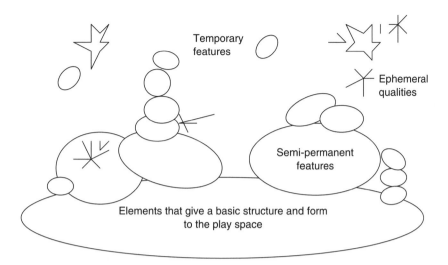

Figure 2.2   Four layers of environmental features (adapted from Casey, 2007:43)

These layers can be described as structural, semi-permanent, temporary and ephemeral.

It's important to pay attention to each layer and to work with them at the right stage in developing the space. Some suggestions for working with each layer are given below; naturally, some could cross between one layer and another.

Structural features

Basic structural components of a play environment (some basic divisions of space, paths, earthworks, hillocks and boundary walls or fences) create the first layer or foundations of the play environment. They provide the overall form and balance that will steer the flow around the space. You would think about these when you are giving an existing space a complete overhaul or have the opportunity to design a new space.

In the planning of this 'layer', you would incorporate basic play necessities such as shelter, water, natural features, space to move around freely and access between indoors and out. You should also be thinking ahead to how well it will support the next layers of more flexible, less static features.

Semi-permanent features

Semi-permanent features are those that we would expect to last from a term or so up to some years. They may be introduced to modify the overall space in response to observations of play or direct requests and suggestions from the children. Features which can be reviewed and changed on an ongoing basis could include:

- dens, caves and hideaways made from willow, wood and/or recycled materials

- story circles and amphitheatres made from such materials as boulders, chunks of logs, tree trunks or custom-made oak

- musical structures – large chimes and xylophones, drums and wobble boards

- fire circles in dedicated areas

- sculptures incorporating sound and movement or 'playable' features, either custom-made for the space, off-the shelf or made by the children through creative projects

- meditative spaces designed to offer quiet and privacy

- lots of nooks and crannies.

If you choose to include fixed equipment or water systems at this stage, be sure to choose and site them very carefully as they will be a constant feature in the play environment for quite some time and may be troublesome and expensive to change.

Temporary features

Temporary features may be in place just for a few hours or weeks. These elements are an immediate response to what happens in the play space and may arise apparently spontaneously. They might be created by the children, in which case adults need to be alert; what may not at first glance look like something valuable could in fact be the result of a very meaningful engagement between the child and the environment. Adults can also be the initiators of temporary features as a response to observations and planning for play. A supply of art, recycled, junk and natural materials is the key to allowing these features to develop. Some examples include:

- tents and bivouacs made from branches, bamboo canes and fabric

- mini paddling pools or sandpits made from ton bags from builders' yards (with the edges rolled down) or circles of old tyres with a tarpaulin thrown across them

- 'washing lines' pegged up with leaves and toys

- water systems made from plastic tubing and connectors from a plumbing supplier

- stages made from benches and planks

- swings hung from trees

- secret dens partitioned off by children using pallets, plans and pegged-up cloth

- little toys and 'charms' tucked into niches in the walls.

Ephemeral features

Those unpredictable, magical delights given to us by nature:

- early morning cobwebs sparkling with dew

- a raindrop about to drip from the end of a leaf onto a child's forehead

- the flood of light when the sun appears from behind a cloud

- birdsong

- a maze of snail trails

- a thick coating of frost.

Ephemeral features really highlight why spaces with natural features support richer and more open-ended play. Off-the-shelf play equipment in a sea of soft 'safety surface' can become virtually unplayable in many weather conditions whereas a more varied natural environment just becomes more complex and inviting with the change of weather and the seasons.

Photo 2.1   An ankle-height work of art

The influence of the environment on inclusive play

While the environment has a crucial role in supporting play in general, it is also a particularly important starting point to achieving more inclusive play opportunities for children. A rich play environment creates opportunities for children to follow a number of paths through their explorations and discoveries to open-ended destinations. Put simply, the richer the range of possibilities the environment offers, the more chance of a child finding the possibility that they in particular need.

Photo 2.2   Magical cobwebs appear overnight

A boring or neglected play environment lets children down by offering insufficient opportunities to expand and develop their play. Because poor play environments give children less chance to enjoy playing together, their play may be frustrated or destructive. This in turn can generate negative attitudes from adults who may blame the children, as opposed to the understanding that the environment is failing them.

This tendency to blame the failings of the play environment on the children can lead to misdirected interventions which may compound the difficulty and further deprive children of opportunities for free, satisfying play. Typical interventions of this sort are to shorten or even abolish play and break times; to introduce more management of children's play in the form of rotas, rules, organized games and zoning of playgrounds; and even to bring in the banning of some games.

Titman (1994) suggested that the environment conveys subtle messages to children which she described as the 'hidden curriculum'. This conveys messages and meanings to children which influence their attitude and behaviour in a variety of ways.

A poor environment, for example, may give youngsters the message that children and what they like to do are not valued enough by adults to provide something that better meets their needs. This hidden curriculum is also very relevant to inclusion. The environment and the way it is organized and labeled may convey messages to children about who is expected to use it and whether it is identified as 'special' or for everyone. For example, a sensory garden may quickly be seen as 'for' particular children.

Children may experience the same environment in the course of their day (arriving at school, during playtime, during an outdoor lesson, at the out-of-school club) but with different expectations or restrictions placed on their behaviour there at different times. Other transitions, such as moving from the reception class to Year 1, for example, may also include a change in the use of space which is implicit rather than explicit.

Some children can accommodate these differences fairly easily, while others may find them very confusing and difficult to make sense of. It may not be immediately apparent to them what is expected of them and others in terms of roles and behaviour in a particular place. This can cause children to feel anxiety and lack of confidence (What am I supposed to do here? How do I join in?) and may result in behaviour that is interpreted as difficult or challenging.

Some children need longer to make sense of their surroundings or repeated opportunities to do so. Children may have very different perceptions of the world around them or different levels of experience in interacting with it. Many children with disabilities have restricted opportunities to experiment and explore at their own pace. Therefore, it should not be assumed that all children will, or should, understand the environment in the same way.

The qualities of an inclusive environment

Looking through a play 'lens' is fundamental – a space for play is not the same as an outside classroom or a garden, even if they share some of the same qualities and have the potential to offer similar experiences. A very useful attempt to define what might make up a stimulating and satisfying play environment is found in *Best Play* (NPFA, 2000). Again, this can be used to stimulate thought on the current or future dimensions of the play space available.

Criteria for an enriched play environment include:

- a varied and interesting physical environment

- challenge in relation to the physical environment

- playing with natural elements – earth, water, fire

- movement – for example, running, jumping, rolling, climbing and balancing

- manipulating natural and fabricated materials

- stimulation of the five senses

- experiencing change in the natural and built environment

- social interaction

- playing with identity

- experiencing a range of emotions. (NPFA, 2000: 35)

These features would go a long way to supporting more inclusive play by widening and enriching the play opportunities available for all children.

The *Play Inclusive Research Report* (Casey, 2004: 27) found five significant characteristics of a play environment which support inclusion:

- flexibility

- shelter

- centres of interest

- natural features

- atmosphere.

Photo 2.3   A flexible environment does not place unnecessary restrictions on children's play.

These features combine with accessibility to contribute towards an inclusive play experience for children.

Flexibility

Flexibility requires that the play environment contains elements which the children can use in the way, and in combinations, that they choose (loose resources, play features for which the intended use is ambiguous). Points to consider:

- that the play environment contains a variety of flexible elements

- that unnecessary restrictions are not placed on the children's play by an expectation that there is a right or a wrong way for the whole environment or individual elements to be used

- that there is recognition of the flexibility the child brings to the play.

Expectations that particular areas or equipment will be used in particular ways limit inclusive play. For some children, the commonly accepted way of using something (a slide for sliding yourself down, a house corner for playing out domestic scenes) is not immediately obvious. When they engage in shadow and light play with the reflection off the slide, or use all the kitchen paraphernalia to make patterns on the floor, they haven't got it wrong, they are not being nonsensical (although maybe that is OK too), they may just be seeing things differently.

You might observe examples such as:

- a slide being used by children to experiment with running water, for rolling balls or sliding sand

- a tree as a den, a 'safe' zone in tig games, a shelter for storytelling, a character in the story, a giant listening ear

- a plank of wood as a bridge, a river, a ramp, a shop counter, a balancing beam, a diving board, a sign

- a pebble and a handful of leaves as treasure, as pieces for a game of noughts and crosses drawn on the ground, as lucky charms, as pixies, as the makings of a garden.

Adults showing active appreciation and interest in different uses of the available environment will not only learn much more about the children as individuals but will be establishing an atmosphere in which difference is accepted and welcomed.

Shelter

An availability of sheltered space provides:

- a focus for activity

- an alternative ambience to those which cause sensory or perceptual difficulties

- the feeling of a safer, more manageable space

- privacy and a more intimate space

- shade from the sun and shelter from the rain and wind.

For many children, the option of being in a smaller, more enclosed space rather than a very open or busy play space is very welcome. Some children are caused difficulty by particular sensory experiences, such as bright light, wind, high-pitched or sudden loud noises. Sheltered areas can be helpful to aid communication when the wind or lots of background noise in the main play space causes poor acoustics.

Centres of interest

> Findings demonstrate the significant benefits of enriching the school environment through resourcing playtime in a way which supports open-ended play around centres of interest. This allows inclusion *around* a focus, rather than emphasising the need to talk, explain or stick to rule-based games. (Casey, 2004: 27)

These 'centres of interest' in any setting allow the children to interact with them and around them. They give children the opportunity to be part of a realm of activity without necessarily having to engage directly with other children first. Becoming involved does not rely on having great social and communication skills. 'Centres of interest' can be semi-permanent, temporary or flexible features, such as:

- a basket of dressing-up clothes

- a home-made maze made from stakes and ribbons

- a paddling pool full of balls or water or crinkly, shiny paper

- a sand pile with buckets and spades

- a tent made from branches and fabrics.

All of these can spark a wide range of play opportunities and playtypes. They provide different ways and levels at which children can choose to engage, for example contributing ideas through words or actions, following the lead of others, engaging in one's own play but within a circle of general activity, taking a turn, watching, leading and joining in with laughter or an expressive gesture.

> The rich environment is very stimulating of play ideas. They provide focal points to meet over and something to interact around even if your play is more solitary. The den made out of a tarpaulin was a good meeting point. (Susan McIntyre, playworker, in Casey, 2004: 27)

Natural features

Natural features in a play environment – trees, long grass, water, stones, logs – are an ideal way of achieving many of the benefits derived from flexibility, shelter and centres of interest. With their visual, tactile and auditory qualities, they can offer a softer, more reassuring environment than a harder, built environment.

Natural elements such as shrubs and slopes help to provide shelter and soften the effects of some of the sensory difficulties children might encounter. They are useful in breaking up a wide or overwhelming space into markers or 'rooms' that help children to locate themselves. These features can be designed to give children a feeling of privacy while in spaces that can be unobtrusively supervised from a distance.

An atmosphere of acceptance and 'the feeling of place'

The play environment is made up not just of the physical features but also of the atmosphere and this has a significant influence on how children play.

The physical environment can signal that this is a space for children, for example through soft landscaping, scale and plenty of loose materials with which to interact. If the environment is full of signs that children have been using it – digging, interesting combinations of materials and equipment, half-built dens – there is an implicit invitation to children to use it fully. Children having their own names for areas within the environment is also a good sign that they really feel it is theirs.

Children's creative output – sculptures, paintings, planting, installations – should be incorporated into the environment whenever an opportunity arises. When an environment is really working, children's creativity will arise out of it: sculptures made from found objects; images made into the soil; bridges, dens, tunnels and mazes constructed.

Clear physical boundaries around the space create a sense of security for some children (and more so in some cases for adults). Some children spend a great deal of time with an adult shadowing them, usually because of concerns about their safety or behaviour. Paradoxically, secure boundaries can be quite liberating if they mean that the child can have freedom to play without a constant close adult presence. Of course, what is required varies from setting to setting and it is important to avoid the impression of prison-like fencing or the children peering wishfully from one side of a fence to another which will only embed feelings of otherness. Boundaries can be made from raised beds, varied logs and wooden material, and hedgerows (a lovely resource in themselves as wildlife habitats), while climbing plants can be trained over wire fencing.

Sensory elements

A variety of sensory elements can easily be introduced through resourcing a play space in a flexible way with natural features. Building up layers of sensory experience

Photo 2.4   Just a small area of planting can provide a world of absorbing sensory experiences

will be beneficial, particularly for children with sensory impairments, and all children can benefit from the richer play and aesthetic experiences available.

Sensory elements to think about include:

- contrasting textures: soft, rough, uneven, prickly or tickly

- light and shade, reflections, shadows, sparkles

- subtle uses of colour or gaudy combinations

- smells of herbs, flowers in bloom, cut grass, mossy undergrowth

- interesting noises from bells, chimes, water, things to hit, rattle or roll

- rustling, creaking, crackling and whooshing plants

- textured surfacing such as pebbles, rocks and sand.

Sensory signals can also be very useful to children as landmarks or guides. A light-catching, colourful sculpture might lead the eye to an area that isn't normally much used, or whispering grasses might help children to locate themselves in a quiet garden.

Photo 2.5   Intriguing natural resources are ideal for exploring

Accessibility

Current thinking suggests that aiming to create a play space in which every element is fully accessible to every child is probably unrealistic and unhelpful. Children will not all wish to access the play experience in the same way as each other. There can be inherent dilemmas in the aim of accessibility. For example, gates that are suitable for children using wheelchairs to open and shut can be too easy for children with autistic spectrum disorders who would benefit more from latches that are out of reach.

Rather, it is crucial that children's right to play is recognized, that they can access the experience of play as fully as possible in their own way and that unnecessary barriers, social and technical, are removed. Observations of children at play will help you understand if they are accessing as wide a range of playtypes and opportunities as possible. If gaps are identified, then interventions can be planned in the physical environment, or through support, planning or resourcing.

> Environmental barriers that exclude children with impairments, such as uneven surfaces and narrow gates, can easily be changed and are not necessarily expensive. Social barriers such as fear, embarrassment or discriminatory attitudes also need to be tackled so that an accessible play space is also an inclusive one in which disabled children and their families feel welcome. The essential ingredient for making a play space accessible is a willingness to seek out and remove disabling barriers. (ODPM, 2004: 3)

An inclusive play environment should be flexible enough to meet the play aspirations of the child (rather than the child fitting the environment). In settings in which practitioners are actively engaged with supporting children's play, a natural outcome is also to engage with the environment to help make this fit. Assumptions about children's interests and possible pursuits, based on their particular impairment or condition, should be avoided.

Continuity between the indoor and outdoor environments

In any children's setting, it is interesting to ask whether indoor and outdoor curricula and experiences have equal status.

Some settings offer an easy transition from indoors to outdoors – with continuity in the atmosphere, curriculum and expectations from one to the other. Others, because of physical design, or conscious or unconscious organizational decisions, make a clear distinction between what happens where. As this description suggests, historical factors are also an influence.

> From looking at the roots of nursery education it is apparent that that this area was initially carefully designed and laid out and its use was carefully planned on a daily basis. It was not a place to run about in after the work was done inside. It was an area in which the children were able to play for the entire session, weather permitting. It was an area where education and care went hand in hand, a wholly new concept at the beginning of the [twentieth] century. It was an area where a healthy body and mind could be developed. It was an environment in which teachers were expected to work and play with the children. (Bilton, 2002: 30)

Many children benefit greatly from easy transitions between outdoor and indoor areas to deal with stress, sensory overload, needing time away from other children, wanting to be in the vicinity of other children but not closely engaged with them, or a very real need to use their body in a more expansive way.

While adults are often more inclined to separate indoors and out, children are more likely to see indoor and outdoor spaces as parts of the whole environment of the setting rather than as separate domains.

By organizing staff time to facilitate indoor and outdoor play and by ensuring that outdoor experiences are equally valued and resourced continuously, outdoor space can be made available. You could try:

- taking the indoors out to apply in practice (cooking utensils in the sand pit, dressing-up clothes and storytelling in the garden) and vice versa

- creating direct access between the children's indoor and outdoor spaces and planning simple solutions for storage for outdoor shoes and clothes

- having an outdoor kit for every child and for every adult

- making outdoor storage available

- using the wider environment of streets, open spaces and parks rather than just the immediate space.

> ### ☼ Quick actions for change
>
> - On a rotating basis, assign members of staff to set up 'centres of interest' before the children arrive to act as catalysts for play.
> - Set about acquiring outdoor storage for loose part resources (a lockable bench or trunk for example) and fill it with replenishable materials such as carpet rolls, cardboard boxes and twigs.
> - Next time it rains, be ready to get out and play.
> - Spend a couple of hours on the phone or Internet in order to identify sources of funds and freebie materials.

Playful environments for very young children

Practitioners should also pay close attention to the environmental experiences of very young children; young children really are immersed in a world of senses. Practitioners can gain a great deal of insight by trying to attune themselves to the sensory environment surrounding the children. That kind of 'tuning in' transforms taking a child for a walk from simply a breath of fresh air into experiencing fields of colour, sounds and smells; it changes looking at the ceiling to absorbing a light show of dappled sunlight and shadows.

Both indoors and out, we can make use of awareness of the physical and sensory environment by, for example, how we position children in relation to light, shade, colour, sound and temperature and making adjustments to suit the needs of the child. Particularly for children who are reliant on adults to move and position them, we should consider whether they are spending their days in very monotonous environments with the same range of sounds, colours and smells or whether we have created enough change and stimulation.

Think about the balance you are creating between allowing children enough time to really sink into an experience of the senses and the times when you share it with them – playing finger shadows or echoing the sound of the wind or lifting them closer to touch or smell, for example.

Whether children are lying, sitting, crawling, rolling or being held is naturally part of the consideration and since these change, the environment for young children should be adaptable.

Consider the following:

- Small mounds and obstacles to move over, under and around can be created easily from cushions, boxes, bags and buckets.

- Surfaces to sit on or move over can be varied – carpets, grass, sand and hard surfaces.

- Light effects can be varied by using lamps, candles, dimmer lights, blackout curtains, mirrors and coloured acetates on windows to create the effect of a stained-glass window.

- Planting schemes can be used sensitively so that children are able to touch, smell and taste plants and probably pull the heads off all the flowers too.

- Materials to manipulate are satisfying: try mud, clay, water, dry leaves, twigs and stones.

- Cushions, beanbags and seating that allows them to be comfortably on a level with children help the adults sustain their involvement in play.

Consideration can also be given to how the play of young children impacts on the play of others and vice versa. It may be necessary to protect time and space for the youngest children so they can move as they wish without being restricted by the more boisterous play of others. As always, there is a balance to achieve, as often younger or less mobile children love to watch the frenzied activity of other children.

Assessing the environment for the opportunities it affords

It is possible to expand and extend the potential of every environment to better meet the play needs and aspirations of children (in fact, the aim for a play space shouldn't really be for it to be 'finished' or 'complete'). Faced with an unpromising environment, aspire to something better and maintain a vision of the kind of experiences that children might enjoy and from which they will benefit. An assessment or audit of the space is one of the starting points.

An audit of the environment is essentially a thorough examination, looking at the current situation. Rather than approaching it in a mechanistic manner, it can be seen as an investigation in which a range of features can be explored from different perspectives, creating a rich picture. Careful observation of the space at different times as it is used by different children is enlightening and crucial.

Assessments or audits can be carried out in the context of workshops, classroom activities or a series of activities. It is unlikely to be successful as the result of only one point of view or any type of tick-box exercise.

Overall, the kinds of question that you might aim to answer include:

- Which elements or features of the existing space should we retain?

- Which elements or features should we develop, modify, repair or recycle?

- What needs to be removed, made inaccessible or taken out of action?

(Continued)

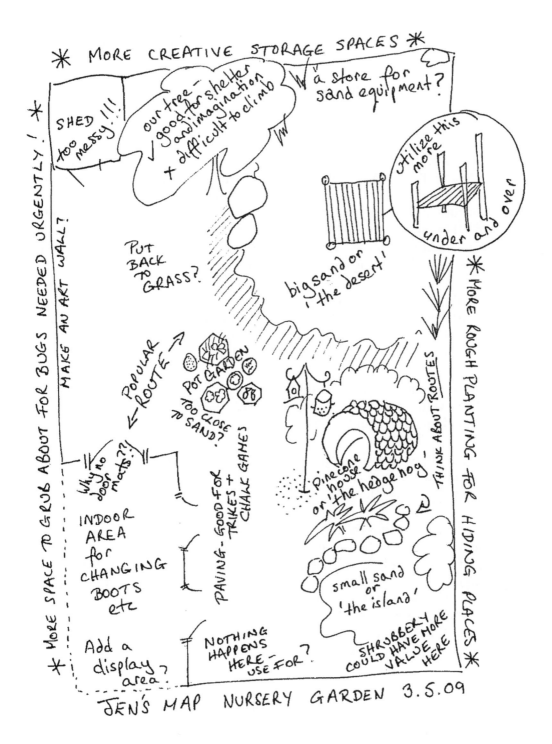

Figure 2.3   An annotated sketch

> *(Continued)*
>
> - Which features of inclusive environments are available in the environment and which are missing?
>
> - What range of playtypes do the children seem to be able to access and which are rarely present?
>
> - What range of experience have we been able to observe in the play environment? Where are the limitations?

Moving around the site with a simple plan on which to note remarks or sketch details gives a fuller impression of the space and how it is used. Have you ever experienced the space from a perch on the branches of a tree or by peeking out from the huddle of bushes like the children do? Any number of annotated plans can be made by adults and children. Multiple annotated plans of this sort make wonderful displays and can be a good way of drawing together the complex layers of environmental use and meaning contained within one site.

Values and principles, knowledge of children's play and the practitioners' close knowledge of the particular children who will use the space are the touchstones of auditing the environment. By including these less tangible qualities, it is more possible to achieve the aim of understanding and engaging with the space.

Asking ourselves questions about the environment will not be a one-off exercise but part of a continual process of engaging with the play space and being alert to the way children do or could use it.

It would be interesting to explore how many play spaces suggest to disabled children that 'this is a place for me'. Do I feel welcome? Can I do the things I want to here? Can I do the things I want to with my friends? Do I have choices?

Exploring these questions in situ with children is particularly useful as the child's response to a place can be expressed through his or her use of it (immediately zipping off to get involved or lingering at the edges waiting for help from adults, for example), by the choices he makes or what he says. Getting out on site with children allows questions to be asked that make sense in context and are based on the child's actual response to the environment. For example, you might ask: What made that difficult for you? You didn't seem to enjoy that much, what happened? That looked like fun, what was it like?

Play environment workshop: an example of putting the audit into context

Aim
The aim is to allow children and adults to participate together in the redesign or development of the play environment.

Objectives

By the end of the workshop, both children and adults will have:

- shared experience of the value of play

- worked together in small groups on site plans and wish lists.

Methods

- An introduction.

- A small group play activity to consider the value, importance and benefits of play. Groups of children and adults are given some basic materials (fabric, ropes, cardboard boxes) and asked to take them out into the play space. They are asked to think about all the different ways they could play with them. Demonstrate to the other groups. Applause! In small groups, think about what children gain from such experiences.

- An activity in twos and threes, including adults and children. Survey the site using ready-prepared maps and consider features that should be retained, adjusted, recycled or discarded. Encourage participants to take into account factors such as sunlight and shade or areas affected by noise from the street. Encourage the adults to listen to the children but also to participate fully with them.

- Wish lists: a small group activity. Produce 'wish lists' for the space, focusing on the types of experiences and feelings they hope people will have in the play space. The facilitator should explicitly say that this 'wish list' is about what you want to do, experience and feel in the play space, and not about equipment (that can come later if it will help to achieve some of the hoped-for experiences and feelings).

- A summary of how the information gained from the workshop will be used and how the participants will be informed of progress.

 Case study

The new 'sandscape' (a landscaped area of shallow and deep sand, with mounds, paths and flexible platforms and tables) has been received in a very positive light by all users of the playground.

It has been very encouraging to observe children who have more complex physical disability identifying the whole area as a place for them and not just the raised platforms that are designed with them in mind. Perhaps just as

(Continued)

Photo 2.6   Children know what they need from play spaces

(Continued)

importantly, the accompanying adults who often control or greatly influence the play choices of these children are increasingly choosing to help the children interact with the environment.

The water pump is a success and the fact that it can't swamp the sand area instantly is a major benefit (children take turns to press the button). An important observation made before the design was completed was that many children didn't want to get soaked with a hose but wanted dry sand to sit in, and wanted to experience sensory play as much as others wanted more dynamic play.

The play team has been constructing big pools dug out of the deepest sand area lined with tarps over the summer holidays. Children have loved splashing around in the pools and there have been imaginative developments from this, such as pirate themes with walking the plank, rum rations from the big barrels and dressing up.

The newly acquired racing sail stretched high above the 'sandscape' gives the area added focus as well as providing shade and shelter. The sail bucks wildly in the wind and fires rain water that has gathered up into the air and down again in floods.

One of the regular children who can be both at a loose end, 'bored' or disruptive has been producing amazingly elaborate sand structures and his mum has been really happy that he is absorbed and happy.

A locus for children's participation

Play spaces should be allowed to evolve in an organic fashion through the children's own play. We are not aiming for a fixed and static environment but one that can change through children's use of it, in a very immediate form of participation. The aim is that the play environment, both physical and organizational, should support all children to access play opportunities alongside each other in the way that they would choose for themselves.

As described above, to encourage children's involvement in designing and organizing the play environment together, a range of methods should be available to them. Allowing these processes to develop gradually and naturally at the children's own pace will produce a more illuminating picture of the children's real needs and aspirations. The practitioners should be alert to the messages children give during informal play and chat as well as through consultation-type activities.

Here are some approaches to stimulate new ways of thinking about the space:

- Chat informally with the children. Ask them about their daydreams. Encourage flights of fancy and invention.

- Provide the children with tools, materials and loose parts to make constructions (such as huts, dens, shops) in the play space. Observe and record their ideas.

- Take the children out for trips and ask them to draw or photograph what they discover while they are there. Ask 'how can we use what we found on our trip in our own play space?'

- Make a large map of the play environment and use a series of stickers to indicate areas such as: my favourite place to play, places I don't like, places I can't reach, my favourite place alone, my favourite place with friends. This gives an instant visual map which you can then go on to explore more closely with the children.

- Walk around the site with individual children as they complete their map. This allows more discussion about the children's preferences and their reasons for them, as you go along.

- Another variation is to give children a set of large symbols which they actually place around the play environment to indicate favourite places, likes and dislikes.

A period of closer engagement with the environment can lead naturally into children's participation in reviewing and considering the findings both of a play audit and other forms of participation. Bringing together information as displays, photographs or

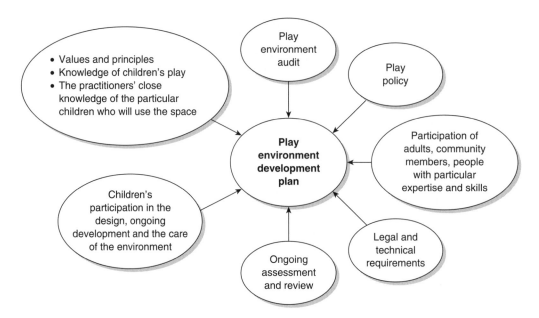

Figure 2.4   Elements contributing to a play environment development plan

large scrapbooks, will help the children review the material and will also make a great record of the process for the future or to share with others (including potential funders).

Reviewing and prioritizing ideas and suggestions, as well as being useful learning experiences, will start to lead to the formation of a more formal design or action plan.

If particular design issues have been thrown up (such as accommodating essential services or how to go about building a play structure), bring in the right expertise to advise. This creates a wonderful opportunity for the children to be involved in identifying and understanding problems and seeking solutions. Combinations of children and adults with technical or specialist skills can result in innovative solutions from which both parties gain a great deal.

A play environment development plan

We have now considered a play environment audit, children's participation in the process and the importance of practitioners' own knowledge and expertise. All of these will combine (as in Figure 2.4) to create a rich picture, allowing us to move on to planning and developing the play space.

A play environment development plan will be unique to the setting, and will take into account the values and principles underpinning the process and considerations important to that particular setting. Supplemented by more detailed suggestions and ideas gathered from the process so far, the main elements of the plan could include:

- the background

- values and principles

- a statement of what it is hoped the plan will achieve

- details of specific actions and time frames

- design considerations

- the methodology/process

- initial ideas

- the people to be involved or approached for help

- sources of help and advice, and technical or specialist expertise and knowledge

- sources of information and resources

- sources of funding

- a timescale for review.

The plan can be revisited and revised periodically.

Summary

- Features including 'centres of interest' and flexibility, shelter, risk and challenge combine with less tangible qualities such as acceptance of difference, trust and permission to create an inclusive environment.

- Play environments are rich with potential and it is possible to give children much of the support that they need for inclusive play through the environment.

- Children's ongoing participation in designing and developing a play space over time will help to ensure that it really meets the needs of its primary users. Children can feel immense satisfaction in being involved through every stage of an evolving space, encouraging a real engagement and connection with the environment.

- The aspiration of an inclusive play space is not that it will have a fixed outcome. Staffed environments have the potential to ensure an ongoing and active engagement with the space that responds to the needs and interests of the children and maximizes the opportunities available.

Further reading 📖

Casey, T. (2007) *Environments for Outdoor Play: A Practical Guide to Making Space for Children.* London: Sage.

Louv, R. (2006) *Last Child in the Woods.* New York: Algonquin Books of Chapel Hill.

Office of the Deputy Prime Minister (ODPM) (2004) *Developing Accessible Play Space: A Good Practice Guide.* London: ODPM.

Shackell, A., Butler, N., Doyle, P. and Ball, D. (2008) *Design for Play: A Guide to Creating Successful Play Spaces.* London: DCMS.

3

Enabling inclusive play opportunities – the role of adults

The adult's role in supporting inclusive play requires a sensitive balance between leaving space for the child's privacy, autonomy and control, and providing an appropriate level of support to those children who need it. This chapter proposes skills and strategies which you can add to your repertoire in order to provide effective support. It explores:

- looking through a play 'lens'
- overcoming fears
- types and levels of intervention
- the effective scaffolding of play between children of diverse abilities and needs
- facilitating communication within play
- modelling inclusive behaviour.

The previous chapter focused on the role of the environment in supporting inclusive play. The roles of the adults and the environment are crucially interrelated. The adults have a specific responsibility to ensure that the environment is a dynamic, changing and stimulating springboard for the children's play. If they feel that a child or group of children is experiencing difficulties, adults have a tendency to focus interventions directly on that particular child or group. Deciding to focus first on the way the environment influences the pattern of play and behaviour helps us to step back and to rein in that tendency.

Once attempts have been made to understand and improve the environment, the role of the adult is often much clearer. It may become apparent that:

- little or no additional support to specific children is necessary

- the way to support the child's play is to build on his or her interests through suitable resourcing of the environment

- there are specific areas in which additional adult support would be helpful.

Photo 3.1   Adults have a responsibility to ensure a dynamic environment for play

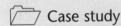 Case study

We pushed the tables and chairs to the side of the room and placed large bin bags full of shredded paper in the middle. At first, the children went for their usual preferred activities but when we started throwing the paper around ourselves, they looked as if to say 'we can play with that?' and got stuck in.

They were laughing and throwing paper over each other and burying each other under huge piles of it.

The children were more interactive today than usual as the paper provided a liberating, exciting and non-verbal way of playing together. (*Source*: McIntyre, 2007: 29)

Looking through a play 'lens'

The whole play environment is made up of everyone in it, their personalities, the weather, the seasons, events in the lives of the children and the community. We have to remember and accept that these are not all under our control. As adults working there, we are an important and influential element in that whole environment – but not the only one.

So many agendas attach themselves to children's services that sometimes a refocusing is required in order to look at children's play behaviours in the light of what we know and value about play and children. The previous chapters have already discussed play as a right of children and linked it to other aspects of the Convention. We have looked at definitions and understandings of inclusive play and these form part of the picture, reminding us again of the idea of children being in control of their own play and it not conforming to rules. Thinking about 'playtypes' is also a particularly useful way of understanding the range of behaviours we see when children play. Hughes, who has led on the theorizing on playtypes, describes playtypes as 'manifested in sixteen different forms that range from three-dimensional movement to rough and tumble, and from exploration of, and experimentation with, objects and spaces, to dialogue and symbolism' (2006: 35). Space does not permit an in-depth look at each of these forms but the sixteen are listed here as a prompt or discussion for further investigation of Hughes' work on each in the extensive literature.

Symbolic play	Rough and tumble play	Exploratory play
Socio-dramatic play	Social play	Creative play
Communication play	Dramatic play	Deep play	Fantasy play
Imaginative play	Locomotor play	
Mastery play	Object play	Role play	Recapitulative play

Structured observation looking out for playtypes can be very rewarding and in general using playtypes as background knowledge can help make observations more purposeful.

Some types of play are given a higher value than others in children's settings. This valuing leads to some types of play being praised and encouraged while other types of play are actively discouraged or even forbidden. Many of the types of play that are not highly valued by adults have enormous value to the children and play a part in inclusion. You might like to reflect on which types of play are accepted or discouraged in your setting.

Often, the most highly valued tend to be those types of play that are seen to be productive or potentially productive; play that is artistic, creative, musical, dramatic or can produce products such as paintings or performances.

Play which demonstrates positive values such as cooperation and negotiation is accepted and encouraged but play which is considered disruptive or which causes anxiety in adults is often not valued and may be suppressed altogether. This can be play that appears aimless or challenging. Playing in the rain, play fighting, play dealing with conflict or difficult issues such as death or gender roles, daydreaming, repetitive play, word play using slang, mimicry and in-jokes may all fall into these categories.

Naturally accommodating play which appears aimless or challenging can mean some debate within a setting and its constituent group. That debate in itself can be a valuable process if it allows the roots of adults' perception of play to be disentangled and for shared understanding to be arrived at. For example, 'play fighting' or 'rough and tumble' has many natural and beneficial aspects – bonding, judgment, physical contact, learning about boundaries, playful communication, exhilaration of display – and characteristics of 'self handicapping, not using full strength, letting one's self be caught and the predominance of the play face' (Hughes, 2006).

Similarly, settings may have a problem with apparently aimless behaviour (and may particularly see it as reflecting badly on the adults if the children are not engaged in specific activities). As in the example of play fighting above, adults' perceptions of what constitutes a valuable activity will benefit from some examination and self-awareness regarding the values that one brings to the judgement.

Of course, we have a responsibility of care towards the children we work with which includes ensuring they are not victims of another's bullying or aggression or are at risk of serious harm or injury from their own or others' activities. We also have to ensure that the policing we undertake of children's play does not serve to exclude experiences that have value and meet a child's need, simply because we do not recognize them as play.

In early years settings, it may be that the play of some children with disabilities does not feel or look quite like the play of the majority – for example, it may seem more repetitive, draw on sensory experiences to a greater degree or appear more fleeting than with other children.

Instead of highlighting difference between children in a negative way, valuing the broad spectrum of playtypes means that the setting will be closer to accommodating children's different ways of being and expressing themselves.

In effect, the proposal here is that the wider variety of play and ways of playing the setting supports, the more inclusive it is of children with a wide range of abilities and needs. The narrower it becomes, the more it excludes those children who struggle to understand or keep up.

Overcoming fears

Enjoying the challenge of a new way of working can quite naturally go in tandem with feelings of anxiety or concern. The fears we might feel are real – but let's try and get them out of the way. Children deserve to get the best out of their experiences and our fears shouldn't be what is holding them back.

Moving forward from concerns to solutions

Aim
The aim is to identify concerns and solutions in relation to the development of inclusive play in the setting.

Objectives
In this instance, the objectives are to:

- acknowledge that the team and team members may have concerns about the development of more inclusive play in the setting

- give an opportunity to express these concerns and fears

- collectively identify solutions.

Materials

Useful materials include:

- slips of paper

- sticky tape

- large sheets of paper

- marker pens.

Method

- The facilitator (possibly a team member) sets the scene with a short introduction explaining where the group is in relation to inclusive play and why they have come together for this activity. He/she acknowledges that making change can be challenging so it is natural to feel some concern. Voicing these concerns will give us a chance to take positive steps forward.

- In small groups, discuss and try to list issues that may create difficulties or barriers in the course of developing inclusive play. Put each issue onto a separate slip of paper. Write as many as come to mind.

- Alternatively, if you feel that people would find it difficult to voice their concerns in the group, pre-prepare a list of concerns by gathering them in advance from members of the team and then carry on with the next steps as a group.

- Gather up all the slips from each group and lay them on a table or other accessible work surface. Group them together into common themes, match up any duplicates and stick them down on the left-hand side of a large sheet of paper.

- As a group, now think about where these concerns come from. The list may include things like lack of knowledge, lack of experience, myths, 'we heard it from someone else', 'we don't feel confident'.

- List these concerns down the centre of the paper.

- Draw arrows from each concern on the left-hand side to where it comes from (there may be several sources in each instance).

- Now on the right-hand side of the paper, collectively come up with suggestions to address these issues and connect up with arrows.

- Don't worry if it ends up looking like a tangled ball of wool. The point is to work through the issues collectively. Figure 3.1 provides an example.

- From this activity, draw up a plan with action points and time frames to address the fears and concerns that were raised.

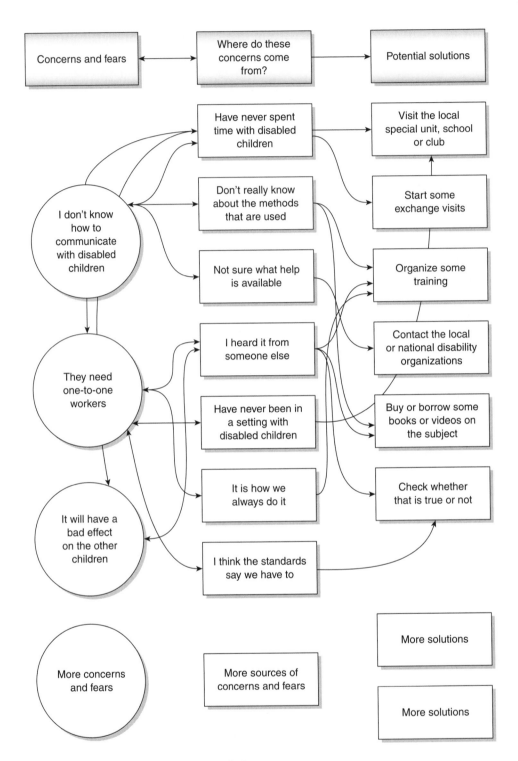

Figure 3.1 Moving from concerns to solutions

Fears relate to lack of experience, assumptions and myths

Some of the most common concerns relate to lack of experience of working with children with disabilities in mixed settings, which creates a lack of confidence and a fear of making mistakes. These can be addressed through opportunities to gain knowledge, skills and first-hand experience in training, through contact with disability organizations and programmes of visits and exchange.

It is also lack of experience of working in inclusive settings which allows the myth to be perpetuated that children with disabilities will automatically require one-to-one support. There are some children who need a high level of support and who should be entitled to it if it allows them to access good play experiences. However, not all children do and some only need one-to-one support for certain activities or in some environments.

Assumptions are made that children will require special and expensive equipment. Again, children who do need something specific to assist them should certainly have it; however, most children with disabilities do not need any special equipment.

Another common concern is that inclusion will have an adverse effect on the children who already attend the setting. There is a worrying attitude underlying this, namely that 'our' children are entitled to attend a setting and that 'other' children can attend only if they 'fit in'. But, of course, on top of that, it is just another myth. The experience of many people who have included a child with a disability in their setting is that it has had a positive effect on the ethos of the setting as a whole. Issues around acceptance, tolerance, welcome, difference and disability can be addressed directly and positively with all members of the setting's community.

Fears of loss of control

In this chapter, it is proposed that for adults to support inclusive play, there is sometimes a role for them to be very closely involved and to enter into the spirit of play with the children. This is suggested because it enables the adult to facilitate, scaffold and support the play in a way which it is rarely possible to do from a distant position.

Adults may accept the need to physically help a child up on to a piece of play equipment. We sometimes find it harder to join in imaginative role play when the children are in charge of the play and we are just another player (if in a complicated role of supporting inclusion by being part of the play). Some adults can become very concerned that if the children see them in this role, they will lose authority or control over the children and the situation.

This throws up a number of interesting questions including:

• Why are we afraid of giving up control?

• What do we think will happen?

• If the child or children aren't in control of the play, is it still play?

In fact, there is a strong suggestion that by really entering into the spirit of play with children, at appropriate times, adults are showing children that they respect them and value what is important to them. They get to know the children better and are more able to understand their experience. Perhaps it will alter the relationship, but it will tilt the balance more towards equal partnerships.

Getting to know the children, their likes, dislikes, interests and talents will tell us more about how to support them in play than will the information of their specific impairment.

'When you really join in with playing with a child, it shows them you respect them' (playworker in training session).

Types and levels of intervention

A characteristic of working with children at play in a way that allows children maximum autonomy while ensuring they do not become exposed to unacceptable risks of harm, has come to be known as 'low intervention, high response' (NPFA, 2000: 16). Adults are a resource, a stimulus and a support to play but do not direct it. Adults can be available to participate in play if invited by the children.

In inclusive play, we have to be especially alert to these 'invitations' to participate since they are rarely as straightforward as a verbal request. We should be alert to children's body language, facial expressions, sounds, where they choose to place themselves, what they are showing interest in – all of which can be subtle invitations for us to join them and support their participation.

Like the invitation to participate in play with a child, the decision of when to make an intervention to support a child's inclusion will be based on a number of things. The decision might be based on:

- how far the child normally involves himself or herself in the type of play

- his or her pattern of play leading up to this occasion

- what you know of the child's personality and preferences

- your relationship with the child.

Try this situation as an example: a number of children are playing in the dressing-up area. One of the children is sitting on the edge watching the others, playing with a hat in his hands and showing some interest, indicated by his facial expressions when he watches the other children. The other children appear not to notice him. Do you intervene to try to include him and, if so, how?

The effective scaffolding of play between children of diverse abilities and needs

A very effective way to scaffold children's play to support inclusion comes from being accepted as a player alongside the children. The adult may have waited for an 'invitation' to join a group of children at play. She may be playing with a particular child who has been recognized as in need of a little extra support and may want to expand his play to enable other children to join them.

Being a participant in play enables the adult to gently hold the play together for a child or group of children when it might otherwise come apart. Children's play can be very fast-moving and dynamic. Full of verbal dexterity and in-jokes, it can twist and turn both physically and imaginatively. This can make it very difficult indeed for some children to keep up and remain with the play of the other children. Once a child drops behind, the other children caught up in their own play processes may just move on without him.

Once included as part of the play of the children, the adult can then use some strategies which will support the child's involvement with the group, such as:

- providing an opening for the child to join in

- providing a role for him

- modelling the play so that it is easier for the child to understand what is expected in the game

- pairing up with the child

- making the twists and turns of the game explicit so the child can keep up

- providing a way for the child to ease out of the play when he is ready.

There is considerable skill involved in recognizing how long to stay involved, how much to be a participant or supporter and when to slip back and forward between roles.

 Case study

A group of children are playing their own imaginative game with lots of catching monsters going on. The children seem to be able to change between being a monster and a catcher just by saying so and doing it. The 'cage' is a spot beside a gate.

A girl named Sunee is on the outskirts and is interested in all the comings and goings but is not joining in. The adult could use a number of strategies from within the play to support her inclusion.

- Providing an opening for her to join in: announcing, 'hey, look, a monster – let's go and catch it!'
- Providing a role for Sunee: suggesting a role that will suit her, maybe a monster-guard or monster-counter. Being given a simple prop may help her to identify with the role (a whistle or mask, for example).
- Modelling the play: joining in the play and characterization but staying within her vicinity and helping her to understand the various characters and what they do.

(Continued)

(Continued)

- Pairing up: 'Look at those poor monsters. We could be the escape team. Shall we help the monsters escape?'
- Making it explicit: giving short, understandable updates on what is happening and changing as the game goes along or pointing out what happens at the gate/cage.
- Providing an opportunity to leave the play: when Sunee seems to have sustained her involvement for as long as she wants to, the adult can offer the chance to join a quieter area or simply remain watching together.

Photo 3.2   Sensitive adult involvement helps to maintain children's involvement

Children's expression of their wish to play and to play with someone else is a fundamental communication. The desire to play is recognizable without words; however, the complicated communication that happens within play can be another challenge for many children. They may need longer to absorb meaning from others or to express themselves, or they may use a communication system with which the other children are not familiar. Although play can appear to be very physical in nature, communication skills underlie much of what happens. Children have to rely more heavily on verbal skill in less interesting and varied environments.

As well as using verbal communication to signal their intentions, their desire to play or their need to withdraw, in play children use:

- body language

- facial expressions

- verbal cues

Photo 3.3   Techniques such as expanding, bridging and simplifying facilitate communication between chidren at play

- sounds

- actions

- communication systems such as Makaton, British Sign Language and symbol boards.

In play settings, there is a danger that the signals children give are lost. The signals or communication may not be assertive enough or fast enough to keep up in a bois-terous play situation. The other children, engrossed in the immediacy of their play, may not pick up on or understand what another child is trying to communicate and the moment is gone.

While it is important to point out to children that one of their friends may need extra time and that this child has a right to be heard, we have to remember that young children are deeply engrossed in their own play process and can easily for-get in the heat of the moment to slow down or wait. Communication systems should be shared with the children in the setting – they learn fast, it can be good fun and will be an experience that stays with them. If, for example, the children have learnt the basics of signing, they can develop and maintain their own rela-tionships without adult mediation.

 Case study

Becky, who uses Makaton to aid her communication, was about to join an out-of-school care project. When the team arranged training in Makaton for themselves, they decided to broaden it out to include parents too. It was common for the chil-dren in the club to be invited to each other's houses for tea, sleepovers and birth-day parties and they wanted to make sure that Becky would be included too.

One adult should not unconsciously fall into the role of the 'expert' communicator. It can happen quite easily that one adult and a child develop a relationship where they really understand each other well and so that adult is invariably called upon when a communication stumbling block arises. However, that may mean that others don't have the opportunity to develop their own communication skills or to put the time into the relationship.

The adult's role in facilitating communication in play can involve:

- expanding

- interpreting

- repeating

- simplifying

- slowing down

- bridging.

 Case study

A group of children are involved in making simple 'homes' out of fabric draped over chairs and tables. It's a nice inclusive activity as the sensory elements are enjoyable and it is easy for Caitlin to join in. The children's game develops into visits between houses and knocking on doors. The child in the house either welcomes in his or her guests or chases them away. When Caitlin is in visitor role with a couple of friends, it is easy to stay involved as she can copy what her friends do by either staying or screaming and running away. When it is her turn to be homeowner, she finds it harder to know what she is supposed to do. Does she chase them or welcome them? The adult can draw on a number of ways to support communication here.

- *Expanding:* when Caitlin's friends knock on her door, the adult can expand what they have communicated to an explanation: 'Oh, your friends have arrived, shall we let them in or not?'

- *Interpreting:* when Caitlin excitedly pushes against the 'door', mischievous eyes shining, the adult can interpret that to the other children as her intention not to let them in.

- *Repeating:* when the children outside shout 'let us in!', the adult can repeat this directly to Caitlin and say, 'they said, let us in – shall we let them in?'

- *Simplifying and slowing down:* when the children outside the door start to play up their characters, offering all sorts of reasons why they should come in, the adult can pick out the key points and repeat: 'They want to come in because they are hungry. Shall we let them in?'

- *Bridging:* the adult realizes it is taking a bit too long for the children outside and that Caitlin's excitement shows she is ready to move on to a new stage so flings the door open and helps Caitlin into chasing mode.

Modelling inclusive behaviour

Modelling inclusive behaviour involves everyone in the setting and, when working successfully, is a reflection of an inclusive ethos. We recognize the need to model behaviour for the children but sometimes forget that they are very alert to the behaviour of adults towards each other and are quick to pick up on the status, hierarchies, authority and power that are at work. In fact, this can prove fascinating to children. Adults need to be very aware of their own interactions and the respect that is given to people in different roles.

There is a certain almost intangible quality that significantly influences an atmosphere of inclusion and that is a characteristic of being interested:

- being curious, inspired, puzzled, intrigued as part of how we respond to each other, to who we are and what we do

- valuing the unexpected, surprises, spontaneity, differences and detours

- seeing inclusion as an opportunity to learn about ourselves as well as the children.

These characteristics give children permission to play with roles and identity and to understand that people have both differences and similarities.

Modelling inclusive behaviour involves things like:

- being welcoming: knowing who children are, knowing their names and how to pronounce them correctly, being interested in them as individuals

- accepting and valuing differences in behaviour, outlook, background and perception

- being a calm and consistently reliable presence

- being interested and enthusiastic

- the ability to use appropriate language and questions as an outward sign of these attitudes and qualities.

The aim of modelling inclusive behaviour is to demonstrate these qualities, not to show children how to behave in the same way.

 Case study

The children are playing with bikes, trolleys and buckets of water which they are transporting back and forward from an outside tap to a moat they have dug in the sand. Some of the children have more assertive roles, leading and initiating developments in the play, but most of the children are engrossed in the mechanics of transporting the water. It is a great activity for joining in with since the busyness means there is little need to talk or explain and the purpose

(Continued)

(Continued)

is clear and easy to copy. This helps Callum as he would find it difficult to play if there was need of much discussion. Once Callum has poured his bucket of water in the moat, he stays to splash his fingers and drop things into it and excitedly flaps his hands up and down. Unfortunately, this gets in the way of other children who are trying to fill the moat and Callum does not understand when they ask him to move so he starts to get anxious.

- *Accepting difference:* the adult helps to create a new channel that the other children can pour their water into so that Callum can carry on with what is obviously a satisfying experience for him.
- *Valuing and interested:* she digs out a hollow in the sand, fills it with water and sitting near Callum also finds small things to drop in and observe.
- *Enthusiastic:* the children are then given the message that Callum is doing something interesting and fun, that maybe they would like to try too.
- *Calm and consistent:* she stays calmly nearby, showing that she doesn't consider Callum's behaviour difficult or unusual and by echoing his play gives him reassurance that his way of doing things is considered of value.
- *Language and questions:* the adult responds to the predicament by expressing interest in Callum's activity, using positive language, rather than focusing on his anxious behaviour. 'Why don't we have a go at a new channel over here? That looks like it might work … what do you think?' 'That's a great idea Callum's trying out. I think I will try that too.'

Summary

- In supporting inclusive play, we are aiming to create the right conditions for play to flourish and, through the environment, opportunities, support and atmosphere, to maximize the opportunities for children to play together.

- Attitudes and mindsets are consistently identified as the most significant factors in the ability of adults to effectively support inclusive play. Creating an atmosphere of trust and permission, so that the children feel safe and accepted, is crucial to inclusive play.

- Adults are a very significant, but not the only, influence and supporting factor for inclusive play. Once adults have looked at ways of going beyond fears and concerns, we are able to engage with supporting inclusive play in a number of areas and with practical strategies.

Further reading

Hughes, B. (2006) *PlayTypes: Speculations and Possibilities.* London: London Centre for Playwork Education and Training.

McIntyre, S. (2007) *People Play Together More: A Handbook for Supporting Inclusive Play.* Edinburgh: The Yard.

Rennie, S. (2003) 'Making Play Work: The Fundamental Role of Play in the Development of Social Relationships', in F. Brown (ed.), *Playwork: Theory and Practice.* Buckingham: Open University Press.

Creative input, playful opportunities

Periodic inputs of creative, stimulating resources and ideas can expand and extend inclusive play by adding to children's play repertoires and acting as catalysts for new ideas and directions. This chapter will look at:

- children's play repertoires
- supporting the earliest stages of exploration and play in very young children
- illustrations of five tried-and-tested ideas:

  – sensory environments
  – selecting games for the moment
  – playing with identity, dressing up, role play and imagination
  – dens, hideaways and the importance of nooks and crannies
  – improbable art.

Children's play repertoires

There are times in inclusive play when children will benefit from additional opportunities that have been chosen with a particular focus in mind, for example:

- to build on the interests of a particular child

- to provide a positive shared experience for a particular group of children

- to nurture relationships among both the children and the adults

- to celebrate achievements or special days

- to add to the play repertoire of the children

- to help the children feel safe and to have enough trust in the situation to move on to free play

- to have a really good time together.

Play theorists have talked about the way in which play begets play: by playing, children develop their play skills which in turns leads to more complex forms of play or, as Sutton-Smith has it, 'successful play experience increases the potential for continued happy playing' (2001: 44).

Play, like all human behaviour, varies greatly between individuals and cultures. The 'content' of play comes from a kaleidoscope of sources – 'real' life re-enacted, observations, impressions, memories, dramatic performances, emotions, relationships, wishes, hopes, storybooks, storytelling, imagination – and it can all be reinterpreted, subverted, elaborated on or repeated with the result of feelings of pleasure, satisfaction, understanding, mastery, control, etc.

It is no wonder then that the play of children we observe has endless permutations. As adults observing or interacting with children at play, there are times when experience and judgement tells us that play has become 'stuck' and is more of a source of frustration or distress to the child than satisfaction. Of course, we have to be very careful about this judgement – is a child obsessed or focused? Are they 'stuck' or utterly immersed in an experience which they are not yet ready to move on from? There is no substitute for knowledge of the child and very careful observation and reflection in making these kinds of judgement calls.

The inputs described in this chapter are intended to support opportunities for inclusive and self-directed play, not to substitute for it. This cycle could be described as observation and reflection, planning an input, using it at an appropriate time, standing back to see how it has influenced the children's own play and reflecting on it again.

The resources suggested are intended as starting points and most can be gathered at little or no expense. As well as having an environmental dimension and keeping the cost down, using materials such as these demonstrates the ability to adapt, appreciate and use creatively the everyday resources that are around us. Once you are in the habit of spotting resources with potential, it's amazing how other people pick up on that and contribute their old bits and pieces (everything from old plumbing gear, to theatre wardrobe clear-outs, gardening equipment and left-over decorating materials).

Supporting the earliest stages of exploration and play in very young children

Most of the ideas suggested in this chapter are suitable or can easily be adapted for very young infants. Some things to think about are:

- *Scale*: think about the size, height, distance and sight lines that will make an activity manageable and attractive for very young children.

- *Objects*: young children love to handle and discover the properties of objects (as in sensory environments below). Be aware of choosing objects which do not pose a choking hazard, which are safe to be explored with the mouth and tongue and which little hands can handle.

- *Novelty*: do you include new, surprising or occasional make-you-jump elements? Think about how children love 'peek a boo' and jack-in-a-box.

- *The aural environment*: children need peaceful moments too and although it is important to communicate richly with children, they don't need to be continually awash with spoken language.

There are particular crossover points between the ideas about environments and creative inputs in this book and the well tried-and-tested ideas to do with heuristic play and treasure baskets. Eleanor Goldschmied's concept of treasure baskets has provided a way of supporting babies to explore objects, discover their properties and make connections between them. Essentially, a round basket is filled up with numerous mainly natural objects which the children can explore, sort, select and discard, depending on which appeal. Goldschmied herself was quite strict about how treasure baskets should be offered to children from the size of the basket to the types of objects, but of course practitioners make their own decisions about how closely to follow the template based on her ideas and how to adapt them for the children in their particular setting (Goldschmied and Jackson, 2003).

Heuristic play, as described by Goldschmied, is all about offering a group of children a large number of different types of objects and containers to play with and discover. The environment is controlled so that it is undisturbed and adult intervention is minimal.

Any of us having spent time with small children in a household situation will recognize children's propensity to systematically empty cupboards and toy boxes; to enjoy collecting items in boxes, tins and bags; and naturally to get as much pleasure from unwrapping a present and playing with the box as the gift itself. These simple examples give us clues to the kinds of play we can offer to young children.

A list of objects and containers for heuristic play would be endless and you'd be looking for a plentiful supply to really support exploration and discovery, but some examples are:

- saucepans, tubs, wooden boxes, baskets, cotton drawstring bags, shoe boxes, flower pots

- cotton reels, wheels, dowling, ping pong balls, curtain rings, lids

- russian dolls, mug trees, wooden bricks

- shells, stones, acorns, conkers, pine cones, leaves, twigs

- lolly sticks, wooden spoons, pegs, rolling pins.

Photo 4.1   Petal soup

Sensory environments

The aim in creating a sensory environment is to transform an entire space surrounding everyone who is in it. Creating it with the children is an integral part of the process. A sensory environment can most easily be built up within an indoor

fairy lights, alien teddy, parachute, glo sticks.
torches, cushions, foil, streamers, space CD
moon dust, sparkly fabric, blackout fabric

Figure 4.1   Simple ideas for a space-themed sensory environment

space such as a corridor, classroom or large cupboard, but it can also be developed outdoors. Choosing a broad theme helps to spark ideas to which people can contribute in different ways. Examples with plenty of scope are: the night sky, treetops, festivals, lost in space, the seashore and shipwrecks.

The value in supporting inclusive play

- Sensory environments can be created quickly to inspire, amaze, intrigue and delight, or they can be developed gradually with the children to build up their involvement in a way that feels safe.

- There is no right or wrong way to interpret, react to or interact with a sensory environment, but they do provide a backdrop to stimulate and support a wide range of play.

- Sensory environments can be particularly appealing to children with learning disabilities and sensory impairments and are accessible to all.

Planning

At the 'preparatory stage', decide on a theme, gather resources, allocate plenty of time and consider bringing in some extra help (e.g. parents, art workers).

There are three parts to the 'making stage': the backdrop, features and final details. The three stages of the treetop theme could be:

- backdrop making: creating the sky, the shape and colour of the treetops using broad sweeps to produce a quick transformation

- features: making nests, a kite stuck in the trees, a beautiful sun overhead

- details: creating eggs in the nests, magic leaves on a tree, the texture of a bird's wing.

The environment should include elements that children can touch and experience. You might want to find ways for children to do this safely, for example by making:

- sealed see-through bottles containing combinations of liquids and small items such as marbles in washing-up liquid, pebbles in jelly, sequins in water

- a treasure chest, display cabinet or magic suitcase full of interesting smaller items

- bags containing selections that will appeal to particular children or that relate to one of the senses

- wall-hangings with see-through pockets containing items that can be explored and then put away.

Resources

- Materials to create quick transformations include: old sheets (can be dyed or printed by the children), a real or play parachute, netting, rolls of old wallpaper, curtains.

- Materials to make features include: willow, tissue paper, tinsel, fairy lights, fabric, cardboard, spray paint, string, plenty of junk, paint, glue, big paintbrushes.

- Materials for the final details with a variety of smells, textures, colours, sounds and taste include natural materials such as acorns, autumn leaves, herbs, pressed petals; feathers, sequins, glitter, ribbons, buttons, corks, shiny fabrics and papers; dried beans, pasta, couscous.

Implementation and variations

- Develop a theme by building a story around it. Ask each child and adult in turn to contribute a line to the story. A starting point could be: 'One night, Joe woke up and looked out of the window into the sky full of stars. There by the furthest, brightest star, he saw … ' When each person has added to the story, pick out key features which can be incorporated into the environment, for example landing on a distant planet or a falling star. A child who finds it difficult to contribute verbally could contribute with the aid of a neighbouring child or adult, with a symbol or picture, or with a sound from a musical instrument.

- When you are working on the backdrop, try to cover up or incorporate obtrusive features (turn a doorway into the magic entrance to a temple) and make big, sweeping changes to the space.

- Divide up tasks between the children. It is fine for children to spend time enjoying the bustle or to move between tasks, so there is no need to get too outcome-oriented.

- The environment can be made three-dimensional with features such as paths, tents, a pond made of foil, a magic circle.

- Vary the atmosphere with: fans to create movement and rustling sounds; lighting (try torches, lamps, candle-lit lanterns, glow sticks); slides projected onto the walls, banners or streamers; taped music, chimes and musical instruments; smells from essential oils and herbs (check for allergies).

- The sensory environment can be used to stimulate a wide range of free play, storytelling, dressing up, themed games, quiet time, music and one-to-one activities.

Selecting games for the moment

Games chosen and planned carefully can support inclusive play. There is a danger that games are used by adults as a substitute for free play when they feel that children need more support or control. However, it should be clearly understood that the benefits and experiences that children gain through organized games and free play are different, so plenty of time should always be provided for free play.

The value in supporting inclusive play

Games can be used to:

- provide some initial structure for children who are not used to playing together or who are not used to free play

- give practitioners an opportunity to understand the dynamics and roles within a group

- give an opportunity for the adults and children to get to know each other

- provide a safe routine.

Planning

Gather a repertoire of games, including some of the children's own. It can be a good idea for the staff team to get together first to try out games and variations to suit their children. It gives each person a chance to practise giving clear instructions and to rehearse getting past potential tricky points such as children losing interest or a few children trying to take over. There are numerous books and websites with lists of cooperative, non-competitive or 'new' games. It's also possible to access short training sessions to learn new ones.

Settings can make up their own games book, adding to it as children and adults introduce new ideas or variations on favourites.

Resources

Most games need only a few simple resources, if any – balls, string, a piece of chalk for marking, perhaps a parachute.

Implementation and variations

- Plan a game or series of games as an introductory session when groups of children are coming together for the first time.

- Top and tail sessions with a game.

- Offer a game at points where children start to look as if they are finding playing together difficult or if children are looking lost or anxious.

- Use a parachute or similar prop to catch the attention of children without having to overtly gather everyone together.

- Be aware that some children do need to opt out of games, finding the levels of interaction, noise or concentration difficult. There is no need to force everyone to join in or to stay involved longer than they are comfortable with.

- Note that it can be helpful to provide some easy opt-outs (such as keeping score, organizing snacks or collecting balls), which will allow the child to opt back in again fairly easily when he or she is ready.

- Be aware of the environment: what are the acoustics like? Can the children see and hear the person giving instructions? Are there distracting things happening in the background?

Know the children you are playing with and adapt accordingly. Simple adaptations to make games more inclusive include:

- pairing all the children into twos, thereby allowing one child to model what is expected for another

- seating everyone in chairs in a circle rather than sitting on the ground or standing

- using easy-to-catch balls such as small bean bags

- using balls that are easy to hear or see: balls with contrasting colours, with bells or bleepers inside

- using something other than a ball, which somehow makes it less of a big deal if you catch it or not – try a lettuce, soft toy, rolled-up newspaper, a vast ball made out of a bin bag stuffed with newspaper

- using simple props to make games clearer – the catcher wearing a hat, for example

- illustrating the stages of games in pictures, photographs or symbols to help explain what will happen.

Playing with identity, dressing up, role play and imagination

Play with identity is an important process for children and one which can be supported in play settings as part of continuous provision. Play with identity deals with big questions such as: Who am I? Who do I want to be? What is my place in the world? It allows children to experience different emotions, and to relate and interact in new ways. An atmosphere of permission and a culture of trust are important so that children are not inhibited by fears that they will be ridiculed or feel diminished in some way for the play that emerges. Playtypes merge from one to another and by providing resources for dressing up and make-believe, a much wider range of play can be supported.

The value in supporting inclusive play

Play around identity:

- allows children to shake off given or assumed roles (the peacemaker, the troublemaker, the shy one)

- allows children to try out different ways of being, for example a shy child being fierce behind a tiger mask

- allows children to safely try out different emotions and emotional responses

- helps children to work through difficult or confusing experiences

- supports a positive sense of self and identity

- encourages children to interact in different groupings from the norm

- supports playing around with gender roles

- supports understanding of what different roles might be or feel like and the ability to see things from a different perspective

- promotes understanding of the uniqueness of individuals and of difference and similarities.

Planning

Play with identity should be built in as part of continuous provision, and resources refreshed every so often to both inspire the children and follow their lead.

A positive outcome to this type of play is that it can encourage children to voice aspirations, concerns and questions about identity, relationships, disability or culture. Resources can act as a prompt to children and it is important that practitioners feel confident about responding positively to those in their care. Therefore, planning and preparation might include training on issues around multiculturalism, disability awareness or equality training, however these would remain in the back of the practitioner's mind to draw upon and inform their practice rather than becoming agenda-setting in their own right. Practitioners might have noticed that dressing up in granny's old fur coat and mum and dad's wardrobe cast-offs is increasingly replaced at home by dressing up in ready-made bought costumes and in many settings by miniature 'uniforms' of police and firefighters and so on. It can quite easily be argued that this is yet another way that children's play is colonized and restricted, as resources become prescriptive than imagination-freeing.

Resources

These include:

- dressing-up clothes from a range of sources including some simple and ambiguous props

- masks: made by the children, from different cultures, bought or borrowed ones, examples made by adults in advance, blank ones that the children can complete in their own ways

- pieces of fabric

- face paints

- some seating, such as floor cushions or soft chairs

- coat hangers and accessible storage such as a clothes rail or line

- mirrors: handheld, full-length, wobbly fairground-types of mirrors

- art materials (felt, crayons, paint mixes) in a range of skin tones

- dolls and puppets made or customized by children and practitioners together to create different characters with different aspects to their stories, personalities and backgrounds

- people: invite in guests – parents, storytellers, artists, dancers – who can talk with the children about their experiences, cook with them, share dance or music, teach a language, show slides.

Implementation and variations

- Truly playing with identity will happen in children's own time, so creating the atmosphere that allows it to happen is very important.

- Over-emphasizing planned activities can stifle the children's own play and start to suggest there are right ways and wrong ways to use the resources.

- A dressing area can be effective in that children can emerge in their transformed state or experiment in private. It is easy to create a small area using a tent, a garden gazebo, curtains, screens or simply a circle of chairs.

- Themed resources can be offered alongside more ambiguous materials like lengths of fabric.

- There is no reason why the play should be confined to one area. Dressing-up clothes can even be used easily in school playgrounds and create an interesting new dimension to all play situations.

- Your collection of resources might include precious items such as a handcrafted mask, an antique puppet or a theatrical costume. It would be sensible to have a special place to keep these and use them with guidelines agreed with the children.

- Storytelling and the use of puppets with children can help to move children's play on or to pick up on something practitioners have noticed arising in the children's play.

 Quick actions for change

- Take a trip around the art, anthropology and geography sections of the library and source out some new ideas to adapt to the play space (try out Celtic folklore, mythic creatures, Mexican murals, storytelling rituals, ice-works, landforms and so on).
- Take a look through your dressing-up resources and replace prescriptive uniforms and costumes with imagination-releasing fabrics, props and masks.
- Set up a loose parts store full of replenishable materials for the children to use in the way they wish.
- Teach children some games that they can play easily without an adult and use the children's own games as part of games sessions.

Photo 4.2   Hideaways always appeal

Dens, hideaways and the importance of nooks and crannies

Indoor or out, dens and hideaways are a constant source of fascination for children. Though the result might appear ramshackle to an adult eye, the process of creating them is absorbing. An adult-built den will probably not hold quite the same appeal.

Dens stimulate a range of play-offering experiences that are quiet and reflective through to those that are thrilling and daring.

If it is not possible to simply let children locate their dens wherever they choose, it should be possible to identify an underused area of ground where children can get down to some serious den-building – areas in bushes and among trees are always appealing.

The value in supporting inclusive play

- Dens provide a centre of interest for children to interact with and around.

- Children can easily make dens themselves from a range of materials and at different levels of complexity.

- Children's den-building easily grows into community-building with a series of dens becoming a village or a series of settlements.

- It stimulates communal play, involving visits to each other's dens, chasing away, hiding, inviting in for secret plans.

- Dens provide an alternative calm space for children who feel stressed or anxious.

- They offer the possibility of shelter and privacy.

Planning

Resources for dens are easily gathered. Ideas for variations on dens can be stimulated by looking at types of shelters and dwellings from around the world, from different periods of history, from different species of animals, and by reading stories that feature safe havens, nests, castles, caves, igloos and hermits.

Thinking through and planning for health and safety issues may influence the type of resources required. For example, should dens be packed away at the end of the day or can they be left out? Remember to balance the intrinsic value of the activity with any perceived risks.

Resources

The range of materials can be:

- natural: branches, tree stumps, logs, willow, stones, brash, mud, ice, bales of hay

- semi-permanent/outdoors: tools, wood, ropes, tyres, tarpaulins, paint

- indoor/temporary: fabric, blankets, cushions, clothes airer, table, stools, golf umbrellas, large cardboard boxes, poles

- props: table cloths, picnic sets, hard hats, broomsticks, dressing-up clothes, torches.

Implementation and variations

- Negotiations may have to take place about locations and materials. Be cautious not to encourage den-making opportunities that will by their nature exclude (dens in very inaccessible spaces, for example), but at the same time remember that a tree house might be especially thrilling to a child who is usually earth-bound.

- Sometimes entry to dens is linked to the membership of a group so practitioners may need to stay alert to how they are being used. But act with some caution. Insisting on particular children being included probably won't help.

- Helping children to create their own dens and using them as a focus of activity may help.

- Den-building indoors is also full of possibilities – from the classic den made from a clothes airer and a few blankets to more elaborate creations such as making caves from papier mâché or tepees from poles and fabrics.

- Dens and hideaways are great for free play, storytelling, private conversations, quiet time, relaxation, massage and adventure.

Figure 4.2   A ramshackle child-made settlement

The children came running in, saying 'Mr Howe, come and take some photographs'. I went out and the children were building a bark-age village. (Sandy Howe, Head teacher)

Improbable art

Play gives rise to spontaneous expressions of creativity from children. The outdoor environment particularly provides children with opportunities in their play for manipulating real materials; for experimenting with found materials; for exploring the nature and quality of textures and colour; and for experiencing the effects of light, change and transformation.

The value in supporting inclusive play

- Using found materials in the outdoors frees us from the limitations and expectations sometimes imposed on specific materials in indoor art settings and from the notion that there are 'those who are good at art' and 'those who are not'.

- Every creation in the outdoors using found, natural materials is by its nature unique and tends to be quite ambiguous. It doesn't have to be representational and so allows for personal interpretations.

- Taking part in outdoor art and also finding evidence of it around the play environment reinforces an ethos of accepting and valuing different ways of being and doing and signals that this is a space for children.

- Outdoor art allows children to experience creation and transformation, decay and destruction.

- It gives children a chance to become more aware and in tune with the natural world, the change in the seasons and the effects of light and weather.

Planning

- Develop a shared understanding that the outdoor environment is there to be used by the children.

- Explore the space with the children and identify areas that would be conducive to outdoor art.

- Think about specific ways to introduce art into the outdoors and how you might resource that.

- Plan for different inputs at different times, but continuously allow for children's own creative interactions with the outdoor environment.

Resources

Suggestions include:

- natural materials: driftwood, grass, sand, water, willow, a nest, moss

- found objects which can be gathered and introduced into sculptures or mosaics: tiles, old wheels, beads, bits of crockery, broken toys and cement, plaster, chicken wire

- mark-makers: rollers, paintbrushes, sticks, charcoal, sponges, mops, straws, halved-potatoes, stones, wheels, hands and feet. (Chunks of foam tied onto lengths of dowelling make good long-handled tools for mark-making; wrapping bubble wrap or foam around the handles of paintbrushes or rollers can make them easier to grip)

- easels, buckets of water, paint, wallpaper, cardboard boxes, glue, wallpaper paste, chalk and biodegradable powders such as flour for making trails

- polished pebbles, feathers, shiny papers, dried slices of orange, lemon and lime

- snow, ice, rain, reflections, shadows, ripples.

Implementation and variations

Outdoor art activities are very, very simple to introduce:

- Take big cardboard boxes outdoors and paint them.

- Draw a big picture frame in chalk on the ground and leave out the chalk for the children to get on with.

Figure 4.3   Easily found mark-makers

- Staple long pieces of paper to the fence and provide paint and mark-makers.

- Stretch a plastic sheet or shower curtain between two points. The children can paint on both sides, see through it and see the effect of light.

- Cover the children from head to toe in boiler suits and let them splash paint onto the ground or onto very large sheets of paper or fabric.

- Make wild patterns by letting the children stand in the large trays of paint wearing Wellington boots or just bare feet and then dance around on a large sheet of paper or fabric.

- Make track patterns with the wheels of bikes or wheelchairs coated in water-soluble paint.

Ephemeral art

- Use autumn leaves and grasses to weave through wire fences to create patterns. Leave them as they gradually disintegrate naturally.

- Create patterns with pebbles in puddles. See how they change as the puddle dries.

- Match the colours of leaves and create a pile of each to use as a 'palette' to make pictures on the ground.

- Throw a bundle of leaves into the air and dance in them as they fall.

- Make a frame out of pebbles or twigs on the ground and create collages within them.

- Give the children an instant camera to capture beautiful effects that they find – raindrops on leaves, the sun sparkling through a cobweb, sharp contrasts of light and dark. Make a montage from these pictures.

- Paint with large brushes and buckets of plain water.

Photo 4.3   The play of sunlight and shadows enhances the experience of drawing outdoors

Art objects integrated with the environment

- Look for nooks and crannies in walls or shrubbery to contain small artworks.

- Make easy sculptures from small pieces of wood nailed together onto a flat piece about A4 size and coloured with wood stain. Hang up around the area.

- Paint smooth stones with colours or patterns, varnish and use to make trails or magic circles.

- Bring in an artist to work with the children to create sculptures, mosaics, murals.

- Look for inspiration from: the materials themselves, the sky, the light, reflections, sensations, how you feel, what you see and hear, cobwebs, rainbows, shadows, changing seasons, your breath in the air, autumn bonfires, crunchy frost, soggy grass.

Summary

- There are times in inclusive play when children will benefit from additional opportunities that have been chosen with a particular focus in mind.

- Thinking through the reasons for particular inputs, based on your observations of the children at play, allows you to assess the effectiveness of that input and to plan for any further support to inclusive play.

- Creative input for play is intended to support opportunities for inclusive and self-directed play and not to be a substitute for it.

- Look for inspiration all around you by keeping an eye open, stealing ideas, browsing on the Internet, signing up for courses. You can find inspiration in: the materials themselves, the children, what they do and who they are, the light, sensations, how you feel, cobwebs, shadows, changing seasons, your breath in the air, autumn bonfires, springtime planting.

Further reading

Cooper, V. and Blake, S. (2004) *Play, Creativity and Emotional and Social Development – Spotlight Briefing.* London: National Children's Bureau.

Goldschmied, E. and Jackson, S. (2003) *People Under Three: Young Children in Day Care.* London: Routledge.

Murray, D. (2004) *Pick & Mix: A Selection of Inclusive Games and Activities.* London: Kidsactive.

5

Risk, challenge and uncertainty in inclusive settings

This chapter sets out to explore the nature of risk and challenge within children's play settings and to remove some of the barriers that hinder the development of play opportunities. We consider:

- the benefits of risk and challenge to children
- observation and reflection
- working with regulations and guidelines
- risk–benefit assessment
- risk, challenge and uncertainty in the context of early years and play settings.

We must not lose sight of the important developmental role of play for children in the pursuit of the unachievable goal of absolute safety. (Health and Safety Executive in Play Safety Forum, 2002: 3)

The benefits of risk and challenge to children

A certain degree of 'risk' is inherent in children's play. Without it, children would never be able to take the leap from what they can do to what they'd like to be able to do, or from curiosity to exploration or from wondering to testing. All of these require of children an ability to step into the unknown and to deal with an uncertain outcome.

Without the possibility of some physical hurt, children would never learn to do things like climb, walk, run, ride a bike or catch a ball. Sutton-Smith (2001: 63) described the 'unrealistically optimistic' character, particularly in young children, of play; the characteristic of not being put off by 'failure' and continuing to attempt to master or improve skills despite repeated lack of 'success'. Young children playing with balls, trying to stay upright on a bike, keeping up with word games and rhymes, jumping over and off things, working with representations and making performances are all examples of play rich with and enriched by the child's optimism.

The Head of Play Safety at the Royal Society for the Prevention of Accidents suggests, with a lovely air of contradiction, that the cuts, sprains, grazes, abrasions and bruises that happen while playing can be considered 'beneficial injuries':

> We must not forget that accidents are a vital part of children's play. It is through accidents that they discover the boundaries of their capabilities – and learn how to adapt to do it better next time. So these beneficial injuries have taught valuable lessons to our children. (Yearley, 2007: 1)

This is reminiscent of a poster spotted on a playground wall where the 'not' had been crossed off a poster, resulting in the slogan: 'ACCIDENTS DO NEED TO HAPPEN'.

Risk and challenge in play are not solely physical and we touch on other aspects of risk (the emotional challenges in negotiating friendships and relationships, for example) elsewhere. The physical dimensions of play cannot easily be separated from other dimensions (social and creative, for example), just as one playtype cannot easily be interpreted as occurring in isolation from others. So while the focus of this chapter is on creating play opportunities that balance the need to protect children from serious risk of physical harm with their need for satisfying play, other dimensions are inevitably part of that equation. The 'memories of play' activity, familiar to anyone who has done play training, in which participants are asked to cast their mind back to childhood play experiences, almost always produces an array of examples of risky play. The stand-out memories often involve being stuck up trees, climbing into building sites and over garden walls, jumping off bridges and playing 'chicken', all well beyond the sight of adults – it's a wonder any of us are around to tell the tales. Figure 5.1 shows one person's memories which include height, water, trees and night-time play.

Figure 5.1   Risk features highly in memories of childhood play

In the UK, a firm position stating the need to get this balance right is now being articulated through policy statements and guidance for implementation.

The Play Safety Forum was one of the first off the mark with the influential *Managing Risk in Play Provision: A Position Statement*:

> Children need and want to take risks when they play. Play provision aims to respond to these needs and wishes by offering children stimulating, challenging environments for exploring and developing their abilities. In doing this, play provision aims to manage the level of risk so that children are not exposed to unacceptable risks of death or injury. (Play Safety Forum, 2002: 1)

As practitioners, we do not offer possibilities of risk simply for risk's sake but because we both recognize the benefits accrued by children when they choose to include elements of risk in their play and respond to the need that leads them to the riskier end of the spectrum. The more overt benefits of risk in play are things like:

• testing and expanding abilities

• learning to judge risk and understand the consequences of risk-taking

• experiencing the range of emotions associated with risk (thrills, fear, achievement, satisfaction, pressure, anticipation)

• experiencing a range of physical sensations (for example, movement through the air, pain, shock, exhilaration, raised heartbeat, laughter, adrenaline, stillness)

• building confidence in one's own capabilities

• fine-tuning physical skills, resulting in improved coordination, spatial awareness, even gracefulness of motion.

Children generate uncertainty for themselves in their play through the 'as if' qualities of play, the unpredictability and spontaneity; children take themselves into zones of not quite knowing.

In their review of literature, Lester and Russell (2008: 20) conclude that 'play may be a way of shaping the brain, maintaining plasticity and potential, and developing a positive emotional orientation and disposition that will enable more complex and flexible playful interaction with the environment'. And it is suggested that it is the very uncertainty that has a role in fundamentally supporting brain development.

 Activity

Thinking about 'uncertainty', 'risk' and 'challenge' together offers an approach to reflecting on what is available to children in our settings.

Make up a simple observation sheet with the words 'challenge', 'risk' and 'uncertainty' written on it.

Spend time quietly observing the children at play and make notes of your interpretation of what you are seeing as it relates to uncertainty, risk and challenge. Try not to intervene unless you feel a child is putting themselves or someone else at serious risk of harm.

Prompts to self:

• Note examples of children taking themselves into a situation or experience of which the outcome is uncertain.
• Note down observations of children taking a physical risk.
• What level of physical risk are you able to observe in the setting?
• Can you see examples of children taking other types of risk (social or emotional risks, such as approaching a group to join in their play, for example)?
• Note down observations of children challenging their own limits – going faster, higher, being afraid but trying anyway.
• Note how the adults seem to be reacting to uncertainty, risk and challenge.

Reflection on observations:

This set of observations can be used as a basis for reflection, either individually or as a group if others have also taken part.

Prompter questions:

• Does the play observed suggest children are finding adequate ways to access risk, challenge and uncertainty? What am I basing that on?
• Does the observation suggest that barriers are in place that limit children's access to risk, challenge and uncertainty?
• What is the nature of these barriers (for example, physical, rules, resourcing, attitudes)?
• What have I learnt from this observation?
• What changes might I make to practice or the environment as a result of this reflection?

Your observations regarding risk in the play space can also be informed by looking through the lens of 'playtypes'. Elements of risk can be found in many types of play but are particularly associated with 'Deep Play'. In his discussion of Deep Play, Hughes suggests:

> to identify Deep Play we should look for children attempting to engage with experiences for the first time. These would normally entail risky or demanding motion – such as complex swinging, climbing to height, balancing over drops, or unorthodox activity, such as riding a bike down a slide. Look for hesitancy and fear. (2006: 42)

Working with regulations and guidelines

Practitioners are in an ideal position to support risk as an essential element of play and have a responsibility to do so. They can ensure that those children whose opportunities might otherwise be restricted with potentially damaging consequences for their development, are able instead to access a healthy range of play opportunities in the setting.

As practitioners, we aim to be closely in tune with the evolving capacities and interests of the children we work with, so we are well placed to take an approach that is flexible enough to respond to the direction in which the children's play is moving and to the particular combinations of children in particular environments.

There are so many myths around Health and Safety, around what's allowed and what isn't, that it is really important to take an informed position in order to make sensible judgements in practice and to challenge barriers that unnecessarily limit children's play.

The most recent guidance on the safety of playground equipment in Europe (BS EN 1176, BSI: 2008), for example, applies to permanently installed public play area equipment and surfacing *only*. There is no requirement to follow BS EN standards and *only* following the standards without also using common sense and judgement would be more of a risk (PLAYLINK, 2009: 9). The standards also reflect a growing acceptance of the benefits of risk – strongly influenced (Sutcliffe, 2008: 15) by the Managing Risk position statement mentioned above.

> Risk-taking is an essential feature of play provision and of all environments in which children legitimately spend time playing. Play provision aims to offer children the chance to encounter acceptable risks as part of a stimulating, challenging and controlled learning environment.

> Respecting the characteristics of children's play and the way children benefit from playing on the playground with regard to development, children need to learn to cope with risk and this may lead to bumps and bruises and even occasionally a broken limb. The aim of this standard is to prevent accidents with a disabling or fatal consequence. (BSI, 2008: intro)

The three basic factors which determine whether a risk offered or available to children is acceptable are:

- the likelihood of coming to harm

- the severity of the harm

- the benefits of the activity.

These three factors must be taken together. For example balancing on a wobbly log: it's quite likely that some of the children will wobble off or stumble, resulting in minor grazes and bruises. The benefits to the children include fun, coordination, cooperation, personal challenge and developing judgement so the risk could be judged worth the benefit.

The principles of safety management that are applicable to workplaces in general are also applicable to play provision but the benefit from risk in play means that risk assessment in play has a different emphasis (risk–benefit assessment).

In many cases, minimizing or attempting to eliminate the risk would negate the benefit accrued from the activity, causing a disadvantage to children which would impact on their healthy development and well-being. The most authoritative guidance now available in the UK is from the DCSF (Ball et al., 2008), endorsed by the likes of the Health and Safety Executive. *Managing Risk in Play Provision: Implementation Guide* (Ball et al., 2008) sets out to show play providers how they can replace current risk assessment practice with an approach to risk management that takes into account the benefits to children and young people of challenging play experiences, as well as risks.

It starts from the position that, while outside expertise and advice are valuable, the ultimate responsibility for making decisions rests with the provider. The basis of these decisions is an agreed play policy, creating the framework for a risk–benefit assessment supported, where necessary, by technical inspections.

Risk–benefit assessment

Risk–benefit assessment is currently about the best tool we have for dealing with the balancing of the need for risk in play because of the benefit to children and the need to keep the children safe from serious harm.

Essentially, by identifying benefits, it is possible to make a judgement about the acceptability of the level of risk and likelihood of coming to harm. Practitioners already make these kinds of judgements on a day-to-day basis when:

- observing and supporting children

- making resources available

- setting up a play space ready for the children to use

- planning particularly for outdoor activities.

The judgements made about whether to enable the risk-taking or whether to limit it are influenced strongly by whether we feel:

- secure in our ability to make that judgement

- secure in the knowledge of the support of our managers and organization for those decisions

- clear about our organization's position on risk

- clear that the organization's position has been shared with parents and other stakeholders.

This view finds an echo in Ball's suggestion (in PLAYLINK, 2009: 7) which outlined the pre-requisites for implementing fully the risk–benefit approach as:

- a formally agreed play policy that makes explicit the overall objectives of the provider in making available play opportunities for children, including the need for risk in play as a benefit to children and the formal obligation on play providers to create risk-taking opportunities

- the monitoring of provision in use

- review and reflection on experience.

A format for a risk–benefit assessment is available in the *Managing Risk in Play Provision: Implementation Guide* (Ball et al., 2008: 68). Rather than a mechanistic method, this approach proposes articulating the benefits of a particular piece of equipment, play opportunity or space; and on risk finding a more complex view, incorporating a range of views, precedents, local conditions and factors, and risk management options. How the resulting judgement should be implemented should also be considered in the light of local political concerns, cultural attitudes and beliefs. How the play possibilities could be extended would also be a useful part of the assessment process.

This guidance tends towards the more fixed elements of play spaces and equipment and doesn't deal with the on-the-spot decisions that a practitioner makes. Providing for play on a day-to-day basis works in a dynamic way. Risk–benefit assessments can take place at different levels for slightly different purposes.

On-the-spot risk–benefit judgement calls

As we observe children play, we may feel it is necessary to intervene there and then in order to avoid a child harming him or herself or others. That intervention could be by way of:

- continuing to observe

- distraction

- redirecting the activity

- providing alternatives

- involving oneself in the play and providing limits (suggesting a height limit for jumping from or providing a way of testing the safety of a rope swing, for example)

- altering the environment (introducing a crash mat, removing objects creating unintended obstacles, removing sharp objects from the vicinity, etc.)

- a direct prohibition (generally a last resort but occasionally necessary).

Reflective risk–benefit practice

Following the observation and documentation process, you or the team may have identified adjustments required in order to alter the balance of risk, uncertainty and challenge available. Interventions of this sort could include:

- increasing 'loose parts' available to children to create their own riskier elements

- introducing or increasing slack space and wilder areas to the play space (areas of long grass, for example)

- planning and setting up 'centres of interest' which incorporate the potential for riskier play (tyres and planks for impromptu seesaws and ramps, for example)

- removing barriers to uncertain and riskier play (prohibitions on playing on the grass or expectations of 'neatness', for example)

- removing hazards which the children really cannot be expected to judge or recognize for themselves.

Risk–benefit planning

Using observations and reflections, levels of risk can be planned into the environment on a longer-term basis, for example:

- building in elements with possibilities of risk and uncertainty to the physical environment

- beginning a process of awareness-raising on risk with parents and other professionals

- undertaking training including playtypes, environmental design, current risk–benefit thinking, study visits, etc.

- developing practice to think through how practitioners engage with risk, respond to it and keep children safe from unacceptable levels of harm

- developing a play policy which sets out the benefits of risk and the setting's approach to managing the balance

- planning for technical inspections, where necessary, to check aspects, such as potential head traps, the load a structure can support, static strength of equipment, etc. (not to assess play value).

> The Welsh Assembly Government recognizes the significance and the value of play in children's development and that children have an innate desire to seek out opportunities to take increasing risks. This is an essential part of their play and learning. It requires us to respond positively by extending the range of environments and opportunities available for children's play while continuing to have due regard for their physical and psychological well-being. (WAG, 2006: 3)

Risk, challenge and uncertainty in the context of early years and play settings

Risk itself is not a fixed entity. Climbing a scramble net is a different challenge for a child with a visual impairment than for a child with an autistic spectrum disorder. Tactile experiences can be very difficult for some children so introductions to sand and water play can be a challenging experience for them. Some children who use wheelchairs find the experience of sitting elsewhere (on grass, in sand, etc.) or being lifted and positioned personally risky. You will have many other examples from the children you work with. Practitioners should always aim to understand risk–benefit from the point of view of the child, not from a fixed starting point.

The BS EN 176 (BSI: 2008) guidance introduction mentioned above suggests that 'the ability to handle risk is based on the individual users' level of skills and not by age', and of course skill in itself cannot be separated from the child's disposition towards risk-taking, their experience and wishes.

The context in which the play is taking place plays a huge part in the level of risk and the judgements that will be made by practitioners. Peer pressure and unintended pressure from adults can push a child beyond what they would choose for themselves (with positive or negative consequences) and children do simply over-extend themselves sometimes.

At times, there are conflicts between the levels of risk one child is seeking and can handle and the effect that has on other children's play. For example, one child may be able to handle climbing quite high up in a tree and sitting on a branch. He may gain a great deal from the thrill of being up high, the pleasure of having some distance from the general play and the satisfaction of being able to scale the tree. This child can judge his own abilities and has a good awareness of which branches can take his weight. You may decide that on the basis of weighing up the risk and benefit to this child that you are happy to allow this.

The context might change your overall judgement, for instance, if there are also children in the play space who would be attracted by the tree climbing but would not be able to make those judgements for themselves and were likely to put themselves at risk of injury or distress (getting stuck up the tree).

As a second example, some children may love hurling around a play space on bikes and creating obstacles and ramps to fly over. Again, you may decide that the risk is acceptable given the urge for speed and excitement. In a busy play space, however, this activity might mean that other children are effectively confined to marginal spaces or run the risk of being knocked down. In this case, the risk–benefit is altered and some management of the space and activity is required, ideally by accommodating the need but in a way that doesn't consistently impact negatively on others.

The same example could be looked at in a different way. If the children's need for speed and excitement is curtailed by the presence of, for example, a lot of young children using the space at the same time, it may be a matter of negotiating fair shares of access to space and time for play.

> While we must act to limit young children's exposure to risks they cannot control, giving children responsibility and allowing them to explore the world in a way that is appropriate to their age and development in a way that they can control is a key part of developing confidence. There is a feeling that, in recent times, there has been too much focus on eliminating all risk to children rather than understanding risk. We must reverse this trend and equip children with the skills to manage risk and make positive choices based on assessing the situation facing them. (Scottish Government, 2008: 29)

For a number of reasons, some children have restricted access to play that encompasses adventure, risk and challenge. In general, there is a trend for children to spend less time out of doors and more time under adult supervision. Additionally, some children will be affected by issues such as traffic, territorialism or racism in their area. Children with disabilities may have their access to such play limited through the lack of adequate environments, over-protection, meeting negative attitudes and low expectations of their abilities.

The case for introducing more adventurous elements into the play environment can be built on:

- a sound knowledge of children's development needs

- looking at the true picture of risk and safety in play environments: evidence shows that playing in a play environment is a low-risk activity for children in comparison with many sports, for example (Ball, 2002)

- the positive benefits of risk-taking.

> Playground risk is exceedingly small in terms of fatalities, and in terms of lesser injuries is far lower than most traditional sports that children are encouraged to engage in, and in any case about the same as the risk encountered at home. (Ball, 2007 in Ball et al., 2008: 11)

Summary

- Accidents do happen and because there are benefits to risk in play, we cannot eliminate all risk (even if it was possible to do so) without also eliminating the benefits to children.

- There is a framework of guidance around risk and play that should support the decisions practitioners and settings make about supporting risk, challenge and uncertainty in the play opportunities available to children in settings.

- In order to make the best possible decisions about risk in play at a number of levels from day-to-day practice through to the planning and design of environments, settings should have a thoroughly thought-out position written into a policy of the setting.

Further reading

Ball, D., Gill, T. and Spiegal, B. (2008) *Managing Risk in Play Provision: Implementation Guide.* London: DCSF.

Gill, T. (2007) *No Fear: Growing Up in a Risk Averse Society.* London: Calouste Gulbenkian Foundation.

Harrop, P. (2006) *Rope Swings, Dens, Treehouses and Fires: A Risk Based Approach for Managers Facilitating Self-Built Play Structures and Activities in Woodland Settings.* Bristol: Forestry Commission.

Working together

If inclusive play is to become a regular, natural part of the setting, then it is vital that staff and other adults work together. This chapter will provide some advice and guidance on useful approaches to planning for inclusive play and involving people in various ways to achieve it. It looks at:

- redefining adult roles
- team working for inclusive play
- supportive (but not limiting) structures for children
- observations and documentation
- networks and cross-agency working
- supporting parents to support their children's play.

Redefining adult roles

Underlying successful approaches to inclusion is the recognition that everyone in the community of a setting shares responsibility for it. Although it is often assumed that inclusion requires extra staff, or that the children with disabilities will need one-to-one assistance, very often that is not the case. The general principle to bear in mind, however, is that any additional staff should be integrated in the team and that inclusion remains a shared responsibility.

A review of the role of adults in the setting, questioning and reflecting on current practice, can be a useful basis for planning and reorganizing in order to facilitate more inclusive play. As Figure 6.1 shows, the views of adults and children can be brought together by asking questions about current and potential roles.

These questions can be asked of children in different ways. For example:

- A 'small world' model of the setting, showing indoor and outdoor space, can be made using simple drawings or symbols to identify different areas that children use. Small play figures can be given to the children to represent how they see the role of adults. The practitioner can use questions to prompt the children about how they see or would like to see the role of adults. The discussion can be recorded using a tape and video recorder, notes or photographs with the children's permission.

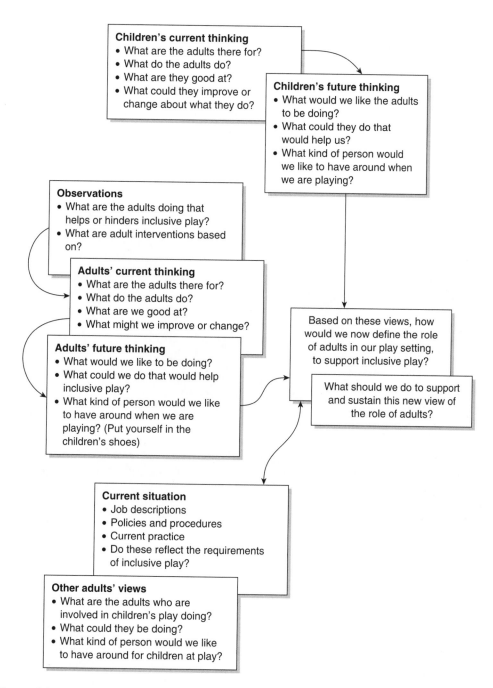

Figure 6.1   A review of the role of adults in supporting inclusive play

- Lay a large piece of paper on the floor and draw around an adult to create a life-size figure. The children can draw or write their thoughts about the role of adults onto this. Again, prompt questions will be useful and an adult may need to capture some of the views of children that are spoken but not written down.

- Take lots of photographs of adults and children doing things together in the course of a few play sessions (perhaps in different weather or when there are different play opportunities on offer). Use these photographs to sort and discuss in small groups.

Adults may find these activities rather intimidating, so it is important that the team has discussed the purpose and method together and see it as a constructive way to gain feedback for the whole team. Equally, children will only really express their views if they know they are being listened to and have their reviews respected. They should be told how the views they express will be used and how they will receive feedback. If the children express views that the team find challenging, it is important that those views are not suppressed. It may be a useful strategy to explain to the children that a particular comment or suggestion will be discussed further and that someone will get back to them.

Photo 6.1   The views of both children and adults can be sought and brought together

Questions asked among the adults can utilize observations made during play. These observations may have considered how the adults' actions help or hinder inclusive play and what the basis of interventions appears to be. Are interventions often prompted by adult concerns about noise levels or rough and tumble play? Are they focused on children who stand out for some reason? Are they prompted by children appearing to need help? Are they proactive or reactive? Are they responses to invitations to play from the children? (You may find it useful to look back to the skills and approaches described in Chapter 4.)

To complete this gathering of information, it is useful to look at policies, procedures and job descriptions that have a bearing on play, and consider whether they really reflect the requirements of inclusive play.

This gathering together of views and perceptions about current and potential roles leads to two consolidating questions:

- How would we now define the role of adults in supporting inclusive play in our setting?

- What should we do to support and sustain this new view of the role of adults?

Team working for inclusive play

Having redefined the role of adults, the team may need to consider ways of working that will support the aspirations for play in the setting. Most important, and often in short supply, is time for the team to reflect on practice and plan together on a daily basis. A refreshed look at the role of adults may suggest the need to free up some time for adults to engage more directly in play or the need to facilitate continuity between indoors and out, for example.

Possible solutions may include:

- improving the environment so that children have more opportunity for satisfying play, allowing adults to move from supervising to facilitating

- considering whether it is possible to free up even small amounts of time to allow for setting up and resourcing the play space before children use it. This time will be repaid doubly by the change in the way in which the children play

- sharing responsibility for tasks such as gathering resources, making creative inputs, improving the environment and involving other people. These tasks can be designated to members of the team and rotated regularly

- considering how members of the team are positioned around the whole provision during free play. Each setting is different but variations to try are:

  o locating staff in key areas but allowing children free flow between them
  o allowing staff and children fluid movement around the space but with a clear awareness among the team that there will always be a certain number of staff indoors and outdoors at any one time
  o locating a number of team members at key areas but arranging for some members of the team to 'float'
  o having a good look at the space to identify points that make it easy for adults to supervise unobtrusively
  o team working and ongoing communication will allow movement around the space that supports the children's play. If a child and adult are deeply engaged with one another in play that moves around the play space, it would not make sense to rigidly stick to artificial divisions of space, providing all members of the team have a clear understanding of what is agreed and required
  o if the norm is for children to be divided into groups by age or in any other way, consider bringing them together with the adults working with them in a team style

- most important is making and protecting time to spend together reflecting and planning.

Supportive (but not limiting) structures for children

Like adults, children may need a supportive structure around their activity that allows them to feel safe and secure in what they are doing. These supportive structures might be physical, such as boundaries, but often also include other types of support. Some children with disabilities may find it particularly helpful to have a structure that is easy to understand and that allows them to frame up what is expected.

Possible supportive mechanisms include:

- picture timetables made up to indicate the sequence of the day, for example: bus, welcome, play, coming together for a snack, play, goodbye song, bus

- reliable routines such as a warm welcome from known staff; familiar play equipment in the same place as well as anything new or rearranged; quiet calming music played at lunch and snack times; a quiet space available to 'escape' to; a reminder when it is nearly time to finish up; a final gathering together; a review of what happened that day and goodbyes

- transitions between places and activities that make sense to children, for example one group of schoolchildren who attended an adventure playground weekly found the bus journey a useful transition from school mode to play mode

- pairing or 'buddy' schemes where children are matched with a buddy who can look out for and support them

- de-cluttering of the space so that it is not overwhelming or too confusing

- a reliable presence and consistent approach from all the adults in the setting.

Observations and documentation

Observation of children's play is crucial to understanding and planning effectively for inclusive play. Observations also serve to develop shared understandings within teams and as a basis for dialogue within teams and with parents and children. Many suggestions have been made in the previous chapters.

Making observations and recording them only makes sense if this information will be used in some way. Observations can take many forms and it may be appropriate for a team to use one method for a period of time and then to use another. Methods might include:

- Team discussions at the end of a play session, where the perspectives of each member of the team are gathered. This has the benefit of providing an overview of the session, to highlight different interpretations of the same incidents and to allow a whole picture to unfold of a sequence of events that might not otherwise be apparent. This method also allows for more experienced staff to pass on knowledge and skills and for shared understanding to develop. It provides opportunities for a team to problem-solve and to make collective decisions about future actions. A simple format can help to focus a discussion, such as the example shown in Figure 6.2. Alternative formats might be more general or prompt the team to think about other questions such as what the children gained from the session, the role of adults and what helped or hindered inclusive play. The team may choose to have a particular focus for a period of time and then change it once it has been explored in some depth.

- The team may decide to focus observation on particular children on a rotating basis. For example, all staff for one day record observations of Jade and Abdul each time they spend time in the same area as that person. At the end of the day, a number of observations by different adults can be brought together. Through this targeted method, a detailed picture of the play of particular children on a particular day can be built up, generating suggestions for extending, supporting or enhancing the child's experience. It may be appropriate to go back to the child or children and check out with them any hypothesis that arose since adults' view of children's play is only by nature an interpretation. For example, a teacher felt that a session in which a child was intent on making a den which was constantly being raided by another child was unsuccessful because of the conflict arising between the children. When she checked with the children, it seemed there was an implicit invitation in the den-building to provoke a raid by the other child.

- Video and photography can also be used (with the children's permission) to make observations of children that can be reviewed and discussed in detail with colleagues or parents. Recordings may focus on particular areas (for example, sand and water), particular types of play (for example, imaginative and fantasy play) or particular children.

Documentation adds another layer to observation, making visible the processes we observe taking place. If documentation is displayed, integrated into the environment and shared with the children and other adults, the process can in itself become part of the character of the environment and an investigative atmosphere.

Documentation shows children that their play is taken seriously. It provides a basis for dialogue and for developing shared language and understanding with other practitioners and with parents and children.

Documentation of what happens in a play space over a period of time gives value to the time that children and adults have spent together. It creates a visible history – the story of the place and time together. It contributes to the 'remember when' factor that helps to build a sense of community. It provides individuals and groups of children with an opportunity to revisit and reflect on past experiences.

Methods include:

- video taken with a focus in mind (one child, a type of play, one area of the setting, adult practice) and used as a basis for discussion and reflection

- laminated photographs and captions, made into sequences, books or displays

Sample Daily Observation Sheet

Date	Number of children attending (see register)
Members of the team involved in the session (staff and volunteers)	
Notes regarding any particular feature or focus planned for the day (e.g. planned creative input, visitors, new child arriving)	

What types of play did the children experience in this session?

What were the influences on the children's play experience, both positive and negative? (e.g. weather, seasons, adults, resources, etc.)

What was the most significant moment/feature of this session? Why?

What could we have done that would have improved this session?

Feedback from children or visiting adults

Action points
*
*
*
*
                                        continue overleaf as necessary

Figure 6.2   Sample daily observation sheet

 Photocopiable:
Inclusive Play, Second Edition, © Theresa Casey, 2010 (SAGE).

- scrapbooks of periods of time, events or projects

- collections or 'museums' of objects and children's art, together with captions using the children's words or adults' notes to contextualize them

- display boards and stands

- photographs taken by children or adults, assembled to illuminate children's perspectives or processes taking place.

These need not be additional tasks tacked onto the busy day but can be seen as a way of sharing in the experience with the children and working with them to make sense of what happens around and between them.

Networks and cross-agency working

Supporting inclusive play involves a number of people both from within the setting and in the extended network. Depending on the context of the setting, teams will want to involve families of the children (including grandparents, carers, siblings), colleagues from other settings or with a range of professional roles (health or social workers, physical activity coordinators, inclusion officers), volunteers, students and trainees. They may want to make links between settings (the school and the after school club, a mainstream and a special school) or between services (play and health, community development or social work).

All of this takes time and planning, but fostering involvement contributes both to the sustainability and to the effectiveness of support to inclusive play. There are numerous reasons for developing involvement, including:

- recognition of play as a way of supporting key outcomes such as the five in Every Child Matters (England) or the National Outcomes (Scotland), for example

- the potential to bring into our settings the benefits of diverse skills, cultures, backgrounds, experience and language

- to develop a sense of community around the setting

- to get things done

- to keep ideas and skills fresh

- contributing to an ethos in which our settings are proactive and outward looking

- having a relationship with the family which affords us better understanding of the children

- children having contact with a diversity of adults and families, helping them to understand that there are different models of families, different cultures and ways of doing things.

Involving people includes, of course, ensuring that disabled people as parents, volunteers, colleagues and members of the team have the same opportunities as others to contribute their skills, experience and knowledge and to participate in the development of inclusive play in the setting.

Children's Centres aspire to providing seamless services for children under five and their families, as 'hubs' in the community. Inclusive play sits naturally with the services provided, such as integrated early education and childcare, support for parents and health. The five outcomes of Every Child Matters – be healthy, stay safe, enjoy and achieve, make a positive contribution, achieve economic well-being – can all be linked to play.

> Because of the interrelationships with the environment there is no guarantee that playing will deliver on the five Every Child Matters outcomes, we can however be confident that these outcomes are more likely to be realized if children play. (Lester and Russell, 2008: 13)

It has to be recognized that the benefits derived from play come from the unpredictability, spontaneity and uncertainty discussed in earlier chapters and so there is an inherent difficulty in trying to pinpoint cause and effect or box play into achieving specific results. Children do learn and develop while they play but that's not why they do it.

There are a number of areas in which people or organizations can be involved in supporting inclusive play at varying levels, from direct work with children and hands-on development of the environment through to joining management committees or assisting with development of the skills and knowledge base of the team. Possible areas to develop involvement in inclusive play include: play environment design; creative inputs to play; gathering resources; practical help such as bike maintenance, gardening and building play equipment or structures; play with children; assisting with photography, video or with the layout and design of leaflets and posters; raising awareness of the issues around play and inclusion; developing links between services and settings; contributing experience, knowledge and skills such as communication skills, consultation techniques, play theory or playwork approaches.

Strategies to help people connect with the issue

- Highlight the importance of play in documents, leaflets and posters used by the setting.

- Give presentations to parents or colleagues focusing on play and its benefits.

- Help the children to develop presentations or presentation materials about play in their lives: what and where they play, who they play with, how they feel about their opportunities for play.

- Assist the children to organize tours in which they lead adults through their play environment, pointing out key features and issues. The children should be given plenty of time to plan and think this through in advance. They might like to have prompt cards with words or images in key places to remind them what they want to emphasize.

- Undertake consultations with children with disabilities or additional support needs and their families to find out about the range of play opportunities (if any) that are available to them.

- Use workshops to highlight the importance of play, inclusion and the right to play (use the activities suggested in Chapter 1).

- Include colleagues from across traditional, professional boundaries in sharing understanding of inclusive play and identifying how their roles connect both with play and with each other's roles.

 Quick actions for change

Sometimes the best way to help change happen is to get on and try it. Practitioners with a range of roles may like to try working together to:

- arrange and facilitate a play session or event based on simple resources
- allocate a short timeframe and designate small groups to focus on developing some play opportunities based on different types of play and report back
- ask each person to bring an example involving inclusion and play from their own setting/profession and discuss
- ask each person for examples of how they could build inclusive play into their role/provision
- for each of the above, consider as a team or across professional roles how you can help each other to achieve more inclusive play.

Supporting parents to support their children's play

> In providing appropriate assistance to parents in the performance of their child-rearing responsibilities (art. 18.2), States parties should take all appropriate measures to enhance parents' understanding of their role in their children's early education, encourage child-rearing practices which are child-centred, encourage respect for the child's dignity and provide opportunities for developing understanding, self-esteem and self-confidence. (UNCRC, 2005: 13)

Parents and carers are of course the child's first educators. Learning and nurturing happen at home in informal ways, involving siblings and other close family members. Playing with their child does not necessarily feel easy or come naturally to all parents and particularly if parents are stressed or tired, playing with their child may not happen as often as they would like.

Families of children with disabilities may spend time in the early years dealing with the social, physical and emotional impacts and issues. On the one hand, play can seem yet another cause of anxiety but in supportive environments, play can also be a great relief and release.

Some strategies to provide support include:

- establishing drop-in or sign-up play sessions for parents and children – be clear if there are any specific parameters about the age of children or how many children can come (and make sure you have good reasons for these)

- ensuring that there are adequate staff and/or volunteers on hand so that parents can get involved in a play session or not as they choose. This would also encourage peer support to develop between parents

- considering that play sessions can be a good time to have other professionals on hand for informal advice or information-giving, though be careful not to appear to have a hidden agenda. If the session is about play, establish that first and then see how people feel about others coming in and who they would like. It might be just as valid to bring in a massage therapist as a benefits adviser, for example

- modelling play techniques and ideas that parents can use in other situations. Use a light touch to bring these to parents' attention over a period of time rather than making it a teaching session

- backing up this support with ideas cards, magazines, newsletters, video clips, lists of websites, toys or resources to take away

- establishing peer support for parents – this could take place during a play session

- taking play out – play is used in various schemes to aid very early learning and to support vulnerable families by taking play to their homes, often through the work of trained volunteers. Look for schemes of this type in your area. Toy libraries are also a wonderful resource. Try linking up your local group (contact National Toy and Leisure Libraries for your nearest group www.natll.org.uk)

- thinking of the whole family – siblings of children with disabilities may need some extra time and support too and often benefit from play time when their needs are uppermost

- ensuring that any information provided is in large print if on paper, free of jargon and available in a suitable range of formats or languages, for example Braille, audiotape or video-taped and signed. Find out if the local authority or voluntary organization has a translation or interpretation service.

 Case study

We decided to run a group for grandparents and toddlers after we became aware of just how many children were looked after by grandparents. At first, we set it up exactly in the way we set up the parent and toddler group but lack of take-up made us realize we had to do it differently. Just putting up posters wasn't enough to attract them, even with images of older people on them. We had to use a network of colleagues such as health visitors to let people know directly that this was available. It's also often the mums who suggest to the grandparent that they should come along as they are worried the children won't get the social opportunities otherwise. It has taken time but now we have grandparents who come regularly and some who keep coming, even though the children are now at school or nursery. The issues that often come up are different parenting styles between the generations, different ideas about discipline, and communication and negotiation with children – they don't necessarily expect the children to question them. Many grandparents are still working themselves so have to fit a new round of child caring into their lives and there are also the issues of the costs of caring that they take on.

We've tried to make the time very sociable, with volunteers encouraging the children to play as much as possible so the grandparents see the benefit to the children as well as getting support themselves.

(One estimate suggests that 60 percent of childcare is provided by grandparents – see www.grandparents-association.org.uk)

 Summary

- The general principle is that inclusion remains a responsibility shared by all members of the community of the setting.

- Adults should be solution-focused and their ways of working flexible enough to help inclusive play happen.

- Observation helps us to understand better children's play and the meaning-making within it, allowing us to facilitate more effectively.

- Fostering involvement contributes to the sustainability and effectiveness of the support we give to inclusive play.

Further reading

Clark, A. (2004) *Why and How we Listen to Young Children.* London: National Children's Bureau.

Dickens, M. (2004) *Listening to Young Disabled Children.* London: National Children's Bureau.

(Both of the above are from the 'Listening as a Way of Life' series of leaflets.)

Moss, P. and Petrie, P. (2002) *From Children's Services to Children's Spaces.* London: RoutledgeFalmer.

7

Managing for inclusive play

Inclusive play flourishes more readily in settings with a genuine ethos of inclusion, settings in which people and relationships are valued, and given time and attention. In this chapter, we will look at:

- **heading towards an inclusive ethos**
- **changing attitudes**
- **creating a framework to support inclusive play**
- **writing plans for play.**

Heading towards an inclusive ethos

The ethos of a setting – the distinctive character and spirit that make it what it is – is evident throughout the practice and relationships within the setting. Ethos evolves from our values and beliefs but is also very much about putting them into practice as it affects the decisions we make, what we do and how we behave towards each other.

Inclusive play is more likely to happen in settings with an inclusive ethos, settings in which positive and respectful relationships are modelled, recognized and supported. The ethos of a setting is not static but is sustained through the efforts of individuals and the extended community of the setting. A general disposition towards inclusion will result in more of the features that support inclusive play (attitudes, environment, behaviour, shared goals) being in place.

In managing for inclusive play, then, the ethos that pervades the setting will be a great influence on the outcomes for children. Does it result in a welcoming and supportive atmosphere; a disposition towards problem-solving; a willingness to give things a go; the removal of disabling barriers?

The habits found in an ethos that is supportive of inclusive play might include:

- giving time and attention to communication and relationships

- valuing people with all their differences and similarities

- finding and giving opportunities for everyone to contribute their views, personalities, skills and ideas

- supporting a sense of belonging

- valuing play highly and demonstrating that we value it through actions that support it

- a playful disposition.

Team activity: inclusive habits

Observe the interaction of the team over the course of a few days and note down some of the 'habits' that you observe. For example, faced with a challenge, how does the team tend to respond? Is their response generally to find a way to eliminate the problem as quickly as possible? Do they look at it from different angles and come to a rounded view? Do they like to see challenges as an opportunity? When children come up with different ways of doing things, are they allowed to follow their own path or do adults think it is more important to keep them on track using planned activities?

These observations can be discussed in a feedback session. Do our aspirations and our observations match up? What might need to change and how could we go about that?

To manage for inclusive play, we need a strong sense of what we are trying to achieve and the ability to create a framework in which it can happen and continue to develop.

Team leaders and senior practitioners need the ability to articulate the values and principles of inclusive play both within the setting and externally. A robust understanding of the issues around inclusive play should be developed throughout the setting and needs strong support from the team leader, so that practitioners feel confident in their own professional judgement.

There are many occasions when we need to be able to state the case for play and the basis of our judgements, for example being able to explain the benefits of rough and tumble play, the importance of risk, why it is fine to play in the rain.

The team leader will demonstrate commitment to inclusion and children's participation in their own actions and through policies and codes of practice. They need to have a good grip on what needs to be done to work towards inclusion in the setting, and to be able to identify priorities, action and progress.

Leadership styles evolve with experience and each individual will have their own style reflecting their personality, which draws on their strengths and the strengths of the team. Listening, giving praise, acknowledging and valuing contributions of different sorts, asking for input and help with problem-solving will all play a part in developing an inclusive approach.

Changing attitudes

Attitudes are consistently cited as what makes the difference in inclusive provision. Working towards more inclusive play in our children's settings therefore implies that we have to give time and attention to attitudinal change.

Changing attitudes is not always easy but there are some strategies that can be useful:

- Before we can change our beliefs or our practice, we sometimes have to let go of a previously strongly held view or idea. It might be something into which we have put time, energy and commitment, for example developing a particular type of provision, advocating the need for specialist services or believing what we do is good enough already. Spending time finding out about these 'prior commitments' and talking them through can start to allow space for change.

- Change happens in stages, steps back, forwards and sideways. We probably wouldn't have arrived at the stage we are at now without the previous ones, just as where we are now is not a final destination.

- People should be provided with the opportunity and information to recognize the need for change and the time to accommodate new ideas. Giving information, opportunities for visits, conversations with children and adults with disabilities, and attending conferences may assist shifts in thinking.

- Not changing is also a choice with its own benefits and dangers. What happens if we just carry on doing what we do, regardless of the changing climate of inclusion or the policy and legal context? When looking at the reasons for change, we needn't be afraid of also examining the consequences of not changing.

- Identifying people whose influence carries some weight and bringing them in to share their views can be extremely useful. These might be parents of children with disabilities, disabled adults, colleagues from other settings, academics. If putting people together in person is difficult, then magazine articles, academic papers or video-taped discussions or lectures might help.

- Try to harness the energy that is put into resisting change and redirect it – perhaps by asking the individual or individuals to lead a subgroup, take on a policy review or gather information. Involvement in the process of defining goals and working out how to reach them will be more motivating than feeling only an external pressure to change.

- One of the most powerful ways of changing people's attitudes to inclusive play is for them to experience it directly and see it work for the children. For that to happen, we need to have children with different needs and abilities, backgrounds and personalities, interests and talents together in interesting environments, playing alongside each other with appropriate adult support. Nothing is more powerful than seeing inclusive play in action.

Creating a framework to support inclusive play

The *Play Inclusive Research Report* suggested that:

> We can rethink play ... by placing play at the centre of a framework for inclusion. By doing so we see that play can both influence, and be influenced by:

- values and attitudes (ethos)

- practice

- the environment

- the role of adults

- policy. (Casey, 2004: 26)

Valuing inclusive play means taking active steps to put play at the centre of thinking. The team leader can put in place: the opportunities to develop a shared understanding of the values and principles of inclusive play; regular opportunities for consultation and development of ongoing dialogue; opportunities to review, adapt and develop the environment; a strong sense of direction and policy development.

Here are some practical areas a senior worker or team leader might want to consider to create a supportive framework for inclusive play.

Resources

- Consider whether budgets are used and allocated in the most effective way to support inclusive play.

- Join with other settings or organizations to share resources or jointly raise funds.

- Establish a budget that can be used flexibly to support inclusion as the occasion or opportunity arises.

- Keep up-to-date information resources (inclusion practice, guidance, web-based resources) and share these with the team.

- Identify specific pieces of work or items that are fundable – for example, training, play resources, outdoor development.

Time

- Create regular opportunities to reflect on values and what they mean to practice.

- Ensure that all members of the team have time to plan and reflect on practice on a regular basis, to attend training and other development opportunities, to take part in team meetings and reviews.

- Put in place timescales for new things to get going, for change to happen and for progress to be reviewed.

- Manage time for change – prioritizing, monitoring and evaluation.

- Keep communication flowing in all directions.

- Manage time flexibly – allowing scope to try out new things in different ways, for special events, switching roles, being creative about staff deployment.

People

- Ensure all staff have equitable opportunities for training and development, both general and specific.

- Build in regular support and supervision opportunities for all staff.

- Bring people in and get them involved on a regular basis, including volunteers, sessional workers, parents, grandparents.

- Develop good teamwork for inclusive play, giving all team members a shared responsibility for inclusion. Practitioners with particular responsibility or skills in relation to inclusion are full members of the team.

- Empower teams to have confidence in their own judgements, knowing that they will be supported by the organization.

- Be available and approachable for children to communicate with you directly and work towards children's participation being a natural part of the setting.

- Arrange disability equality training for all members of the team including managers and committee members. Equal opportunities should be about ways of working and more than simply the contents of a forgotten, shelved document.

- Arrange an ongoing programme of training around equality issues for all members of the team.

- Be rigorous about equal opportunities in recruitment and selection of staff.

- Get sussed about employing disabled people. The Sure Start Unit has produced a range of resources, including publications and free downloads, with advice on developing successful recruitment campaigns.

  There is a good business case for employing disabled people. If you don't, you are missing out on a huge pool of potential employees with a wide range of skills and abilities. Disabled people are equally as capable as their non-disabled colleagues. And they often bring exceptional and complementary talents to the job. Introducing all children to disability from an early age will help encourage their appreciation of diversity. And, especially for disabled children, disabled adults can provide valuable role models. (DfES, 2004: 6)

Stimulating development

- Ensure basic needs in the team are met, such as the need for security, respect, trust, appreciation, opportunities to develop and to be heard.

- Bring in people with specific expertise or experience.

- Motivate teams – ensure that members of the team can see their contribution and that it is recognized.

- Work towards quality standards and quality assurance schemes as a way of developing the provision and motivating teams.

- Encourage open and forward-looking thinking and an investigative atmosphere, and remind the team that what you are doing links in with bigger issues and questions in society.

Building bridges and partnerships

- Build strong links in the community. Seek out the other people in your area who are working in play or inclusion.

- Make contact with the umbrella organizations and national bodies.

- Tap into existing networks, locally or nationally – consider relevant types of networks such as disabled people's organizations, parent-led or environment-focused networks.

- Make sure there is time for building relationships with parents.

- Find out how your work and interests compare to that of other professionals.

- Make links to encourage all the settings locally, which children do or could attend, to share experience and work more inclusively, giving children a range of accessible options for play.

Plans and policies

- Keep policies (such as admission policies) under review to identify any discriminatory clauses and take steps to rewrite or amend them. Questions might be asked such as: Are staff aware of the policy or procedure and do they know how to use it? Is it accessible in language and format? Has it been carefully thought out so that it does not inadvertently discriminate against any groups? Is it clear who is responsible for doing what and when and how they do it? How will it be recorded? Does it help the delivery of a service in line with aspirations, legislation and standards?

- Ensure that statements regarding inclusion are on every significant document and are integral to all job descriptions.

- Ensure that there are a range of ways and levels for children to be involved in influencing and participating in decision-making processes.

- Consider who is actively involved in running and developing the setting. Are the voices of children, colleagues and parents heard?

- Take a proactive approach to providing for the benefits of risk and challenge in play with robust statements of benefits and solidly based risk assessments.

Notice play and celebrate it

- Make an annual award in the setting for the person who has made a significant contribution to inclusive play.

- Organize days devoted to inclusive play when you invite others to share the experience.

- Document and share good practice.

- Develop submissions for external awards.

- Highlight play in your leaflets, documents and policies.

- Recognize progress – have the staff team evolved a more flexible style? Are the children getting a say? Has a disabling barrier been identified and removed?

- Say thank you.

Writing plans for play

The process of developing a play policy and strategy in children's settings brings a new focus on play, allowing it to be better understood, planned for and developed. Although play is a distinct concept, the benefits and impact of play cut across a large number of areas including health, education, physical activity, social relationships, therapeutic practice, behaviour, emotional health and well-being. Play is often considered separately as an element of each of these rather than as a primary focus (as it would be for the children). A play policy and strategy enables these strands and the people with an interest in them to be brought together, to consider play in a coherent fashion with play at the centre.

The benefits of developing play policies and strategies in children's settings include:

- bringing together people from different professional backgrounds with a common interest in play

- allowing for the development of a common understanding of play, a shared value base and agreement on definitions of play (children's rights, article 31, the importance of a range of play, importance of play to children with disabilities, risk)

- supporting the participation of children

- developing a deeper understanding of play and greater specific knowledge about the play environment and culture of the setting

- greater understanding of how the roles of different members of the community of the setting can complement each other in supporting the objectives of the play strategy

- more children accessing more satisfying and wider-ranging play experiences

- the removal of disabling barriers

- inclusive practices and procedures

- an inclusive environment and design

- less adult intervention in play and more effective support where it is required

- sustainability.

The scope of the play policy and strategy depends on the type and scale of the provision, however there are a number of common principles which will underlie the development of a strategy for play, including non-discrimination and the right to play, as expressed by the UNCRC.

The process of developing these is an opportunity to put ideas about participation into practice. It is an area which will attract the interest and views of children and adults who have different types and levels of involvement. The process may include:

- establishing a steering group or review group which includes children and adults

- bringing in advice or support from external organizations (for example, a play development officer or an experienced children's consultant)

- identifying one or two people with lead responsibility (overall or in specific areas) to listen, gather views and prepare drafts

- establishing key principles which will underlie the strategy and developing a common understanding of play (through discussion, activities such as those in previous chapters, inputs from experienced play practitioners)

- an audit of current provision and opportunities, taking into account issues around quality, environment (see Chapter 2), adults (see Figure 6.1), usage, accessibility

- gathering and reviewing legislation, policies, standards and strategies with a bearing on play in the particular setting

- wide engagement with all the children in the setting who wish to participate and consultation with children who are potential users but currently are excluded or uninvolved

- consultation with adults in the setting such as janitors, classroom assistants, support staff, parents, speech therapists, physiotherapists, occupational therapists; people from other settings which the children use – nursery, after school club, breakfast club, play scheme, classroom – to promote partnerships and consistency

- gathering together information, drawing out key themes and issues

- the identification of objectives

- preparation of the draft strategy and consultation

- agreement of the strategy and development of dissemination and action plans.

A timeframe should be established for each stage of the process, allowing plenty of time for involving people but ensuring that there is still a sense of 'moving on'. Nobody wants to be involved in endless meetings. Preparing an agenda, chairing meetings reasonably briskly, bringing concise information and having a clear purpose for each will help. Meetings intended to develop understanding and provoke discussion can be creative, purposeful and playful to support everyone's full participation. Activities such as gathering information or consultation can be delegated to individuals or small groups in between main gatherings.

The final strategy may be structured as follows:

- a broad statement of principles (vision and rationale)

- the context of the setting (for example, geographical, community make-up, policy context)

- the results of the audit of existing provision

- a summary of consultations with children and adults

- an analysis and identification of priorities and objectives. (Adapted from Mayor of London, 2004: 51)

The strategy might also be supplemented by:

- indications of the need for action plans, codes of practice or supporting guidance in relation to specific points

- plans to ensure the strategy is widely known among all members of the community of the setting, including the children

- plans to ensure that the strategy is embedded in practice (for example, will the strategy be included in whole-setting review processes, self-evaluation, record-keeping, and as a standing point on agendas?).

Summary

- The management of a setting plays a crucial role in establishing the ethos, the resulting practice and in turn the overall environment for play opportunities in the setting.

- Valuing inclusive play means taking active steps to put play at the centre of thinking. It requires a shift in attitudes and values and has to be matched by policies and practices that support it.

- The process of developing a play policy in children's settings brings a new focus on play, allowing it to be better understood and developed in a coherent fashion with play at the centre.

- Nothing is more powerful in changing attitudes than actually experiencing inclusive play happening.

Further reading

Council for Disabled Children (2004) *The Dignity of Risk.* London: Council for Disabled Children.

Douch, P. (2002) *It Doesn't Just Happen: Inclusive Management for Inclusive Play.* London: Kidsactive.

Afterword

I have a strong memory from my time as a playworker in an adventure playground. We were sitting outside in the playground quietly chatting over a picnic in the sunshine with a group from a special school. One girl came towards me, eyes shining, with her hands cupped around something she had found. She came over to me and brought her hands close to my face so that I could see it better. I was expecting a lovely flower or perhaps a butterfly so peered in but as she opened her hands an angry late-summer wasp burst out, bounced off my nose and flew away.

I remember it so vividly because the girl had no intention other than to share her pleasure in what she had found. She hadn't yet acquired any fear or disgust of the wasp.

It reminds me that, for children, the natural world allows them infinite ways to find for themselves the kinds of experiences they need.

Remembering itself is such an important thing. We turn over old memories and look at them in the different lights of experience and time, and some of them can come back with startling clarity. Memories of play have a particular tendency to jump back to life.

One of the challenges for us is that play does its own thing – thank goodness – no matter what the current policy or framework, strategy or definition might be. If you are interested in play and are one of those people who can really tune into playfulness when you see it, then you will probably get there.

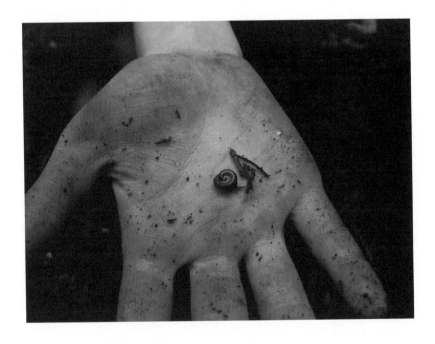

Resources

This section provides information on the following:

- national and international play organizations

- useful organizations – play, inclusion and environments

- children's rights

- play resources

- toys and specialist equipment

- advice on sources of funding

- volunteering.

National and international play organizations

The International Play Association: Promoting the Child's Right to Play (IPA)
www.ipaworld.org

IPA's worldwide network promotes the importance of play in child development, facilitates inter-disciplinary exchange and action, and brings a child perspective to policy development throughout the world.

As well as providing a host of information on international initiatives for children's play rights throughout this site, you can link up to play organizations around the world.

Play England
8 Wakley Street
London EC1V 7QE
Tel: 020 7843 6016
www.ncb.org.uk/cpc

Play Scotland
Midlothian Innovation Centre
Roslin
Midlothian EH25 9RE
Tel: 0131 440 9070
www.playscotland.org

PlayBoard
59–65 York Street
Belfast BT15 1AA
Tel: 028 9080 3380

Play Wales
Baltic House
Mount Stuart Square
Cardiff CF10 5FH
Tel: 029 2048 6050
www.playwales.org.uk

Useful organizations – play, inclusion and environments

Centre for Accessible Environments
Tel/Textphone: 020 7840 0125
www.cae.org.uk
Has a focus on inclusive design in the built environment.

Kids: working with disabled children, young people and their families
www.kids.org.uk
The Playwork Inclusion Project at Kids offers strategic development,
information and guidance on inclusive play and childcare.

Learning through Landscapes
Tel: 01962 846258
www.ltl.org.uk
Helps schools and early years settings make the most of their outdoor
spaces for play and learning.

Grounds for Learning
Tel: 01786 445922
www.gflscotland.org.uk
Helps Scottish schools and early years settings make the most of their outdoor
spaces for play and learning.

National Association of Toy and Leisure Libraries (NATLL)
Tel: 020 7387 9592
www.natll.org.uk
The national body for toy and leisure libraries in the UK.

Groundwork UK
Tel: 020 7922 1230
www.groundwork.org.uk
Supports communities in need, to help improve the quality of people's lives,
their prospects and potential and the places where they live, work and play.

Early Years – the organization for young children
Tel: 028 9066 2825
www.early-years.org
An early years organization in Northern Ireland, formerly the NIPPA.

PLAYLINK
Tel: 020 7720 2452
www.playlink.org.uk
An independent play and informal leisure consultancy working in the areas of design, planning, policy and strategy.

Pre-School Learning Alliance
Tel: 020 7833 0991
www.pre-school.org.uk
An educational charity specializing in the early years.

The Forestry Commission
www.forestry.gov.uk/
Try putting 'play' into the Forestry Commission website search engine to find some inspiring and adaptable ideas and resources.

Early Support
www.earlysupport.org.uk
The government programme to achieve better coordinated, family-focused services for young disabled children and their families. Provides a good source of information.

Natural Learning Initiative
(NLI), USA
www.naturalearning.org
Promotes the importance of the natural environment in children's daily experience through creating stimulating environments.

RoSPA (Royal Society for the Prevention of Accients) Play Safety
Tel: 01367 244600
www.rospa.org.uk/playsafety

SkillsActive Playwork Unit
Tel: 020 7632 2000
www.playwork.org.uk
Is involved in the development of playwork training and education.

Sure Start Unit
www.surestart.gov.uk
The Sure Start Unit produces a range of very useful publications which can also be downloaded from their website.

Every Child Matters
www.dcsf.gov.uk/everychildmatters/about/

Council for Disabled Children, National
Children's Bureau
Tel: 020 7843 6000
www.ncb.org.uk

Children's rights

The United Nations Convention on the Rights of the Child is available from The Stationery Office or can be downloaded from UNICEF at www.unicef.org/crc

The Office of the United Nations High Commissioner for Human Rights
www2.ohchr.org
Click on 'Human rights bodies' to find the Committee on the Rights of the Child.

Children's Rights Information Network
www.crin.org/
A global network coordinating information and promoting action on child rights.

Equality and Human Rights Commission
Tel: 08457 622 633
Textphone: 08457 622 644
Fax: 08457 778 878
www.equalityhumanrights.com
An independent statutory body established to help eliminate discrimination, reduce inequality and protect human rights.

UNICEF UK's youth website
www.therightssite.org.uk/

Children's commissioners are a great source of child-friendly posters and leaflets and may have specific resources (research reports etc.) related to play and inclusion.

Scotland's Commissioner for Children and Young People (SCCYP)
www.sccyp.org.uk

Northern Ireland Commissioner for Children and Young People (NICCY)
www.niccy.org

The Children's Commissioner for Wales
www.childcomwales.org.uk

The Children's Commissioner for England
www.11million.org.uk

Play resources

Many interesting resources for play can be gathered up very easily and cheaply. The following are good sources of recycled, reclaimed, multicultural and generally interesting and unusual resources and ideas:

- Scrap stores collect safe re-useable waste from businesses and then provide them at low cost as a service to members. Scrap stores are usually an amazing source of fantastic recycled materials and creative ideas. The easiest way to find a local scrap store is using the Internet or asking around locally.

- Development Education Centres aim to raise the profile of global issues. You can find a local centre by using this website: www.dea.org.uk

Table 1 Resources and sources

Play	Suggestions	Suggested sources
Dressing up Identity play	Fabric, hats, uniforms, theatrical costumes, everyday items, scarves, feather boas, fans, masks, face paints	Charity shops and jumble sales Letters sent out to parents Fabric shops Letters sent out to theatre companies, uniformed organizations (police, fire brigade, Brownies), businesses (hard hats, boiler suits, reflective jackets)
Games	Balls, strings, chalk for markings, a parachute, books of games	Local shops for resources Parents and grandparents who may be able to share games they remember Bookshops and websites for ideas
Dens	Semi-permanent/outdoors: tools, wood, ropes, planks, tyres, branches, etc. Temporary/indoor: fabric, blankets, cushions, tables, stools	Local parks or forestry department for branches and logs Work being carried out in woodlands and parks or even gardens and asking for donations Letters sent out to parents requesting donations Furnishing stores Timber merchants
Sand and water	Buckets, spades, plumbing tubes and pipes, carts, guttering	DIY stores Hardware shops Builders merchants
Art	Rollers, paintbrushes, wallpaper, cardboard boxes	DIY shops Art and craft suppliers Factory off-cuts and ends of rolls Electrical stores (for large boxes) Scrap stores
Sensory environments	Old sheets, parachute, netting, rolls of wallpaper, curtains, willow, tissue paper, tinsel, fairy lights, fabric, cardboard, spray paint, glue, big paintbrushes, sequins, glitter, ribbons, buttons, shiny gift bags, bubble wrap, corks, shiny fabrics and papers, dried beans, pasta, couscous	DIY shops Haberdashery shops Supermarkets Charity shops 'One world' shops Music shops Craft shops Home stores Outdoors Scrap stores
Wheeled play	Wheels, castors, axles, bells, reflectors Old tyres Velcro to make foot straps	DIY stores Bike shops, toy stores Tyre-fitting companies Haberdashery or craft shops
Creating small areas	Plastic garden gazebo, tent, a shower curtain, garden shed, sheets over a climbing frame	DIY and home stores Camping shops Letter to army (tents)
Toys and games from various countries and cultures	Traditional crafts, games, toys, customs and stories, everyday items such as cooking utensils, typical clothing fabrics	Toy library items for hire 'One world' or fair-trade shops Development education centres Local museum items for hire Local families from different cultures who could bring in examples Internet sites Families planning a trip could be given a small budget and asked for small items to bring back
Outdoor storage	Sheds Old shipping containers Purpose-built storage	DIY stores Shipping companies Specialist storage firms

- Try looking in 'one world' or 'fair trade' shops.

- Also worth a browse for play resources, positive images of culture, international perspectives and children's rights are:

  - www.newint.org/shop
  - www.traidcraftshop.co.uk
  - www.oxfam.org.uk/

The resources suggested in Table 1 are intended as starting points based on the use of natural and recycled materials and materials that can be easily gathered through requests to parents or bought cheaply. You should always use some judgement to ensure that resources are suitable before giving them to children. In particular, pay attention to small loose parts, which may pose a choking hazard, or potential triggers of allergies.

Toys and specialized equipment

- The Good Toy Guide is published annually by the National Association of Toy and Leisure Libraries. Toys are tested by both adults and children with nominations for innovation and inclusion. See NATLL details above.

- The Royal National Institute of Blind People has a good online shop – see www.rnib.org.uk

- The Child Accident Prevention Trust produces a number of safety leaflets including *How Safe Are Your Child's Toys?*

There are many companies offering specialist equipment that can be integrated into a play setting. The best of these can be found through recommendations and it is fairly easy to do an initial trawl online. Ask for catalogues and always compare prices and services before buying specialist equipment. Most importantly, make sure you get the items that are right for the particular children who will use them. It is possible to spend lavishly on specialized equipment but often not necessary. When purchasing expensive equipment such as specialized bikes, ask if it is possible to test them out before purchasing.

Similarly, there may be particular pieces of outdoor fixed play equipment you would like to add to a play environment and there are many suppliers with a range of services ready to sell you these. Ask if there is a site nearby where their equipment is already installed so the children can test it out for real and find out about guarantees and after service. Be sure to look at the latest guidance issued on design and risk (see Chapters 2 and 5).

Advice on sources of funding

If you are a member of any of the umbrella bodies or national organizations, you may be entitled to use software packages that help you search for suitable sources of funds for your project in your area.

Other websites offering funding information are:

www.lotteryfunding.org.uk/
This is the joint website run by all Lottery funders in the UK. This site allows you to search information on current funding programmes across the UK.

www.dsc.org.uk
The Directory of Social Change (DSC) is a publisher of books and periodicals on fundraising and funding sources. It is a national charity providing training, research and publication. Information on grant-making trusts is available on CD-ROM and from its website.

www.funderfinder.org.uk
FunderFinder is a charity that produces useful software and other resources for grant-seekers.

www.volresource.org.uk
This is a free source of useful information on anything to do with running a voluntary organization (whether a community group, charity or other non-profit body).

www.green-space.org.uk/resources
This section of the GreenSpace website provides useful guidance notes and tips for raising funds.

Members of Grounds for Learning and Learning through Landscapes (see addresses above) can download funding information from their websites.

Volunteering

Volunteering information around the UK can be found at the following websites:
England – www.volunteering.org.uk
Northern Ireland – www.volunteering-ni.org
Wales – www.wcva.org.uk
Scotland – www.vds.org.uk

Bibliography

Adams, S., Alexander, E., Drummond, M. and Moyles, J. (2004) *Inside the Foundation Stage: Recreating the Reception Year.* London: Association of Teachers and Lecturers.

Armitage, M. (2001) 'The Ins and Outs of the School Playground: Children's Use of "Play Places"', in J.C. Bishop and M. Curtis (eds) *Play Today in the Primary School Playground.* Philadelphia, PA: Open University Press.

Ball, D.J. (2002) *Playgrounds: Risks, Benefits and Choices.* London: Health and Safety Executive.

Ball, D., Gill, T. and Spiegal, B. (2008) *Managing Risk in Play Provision: Implementation Guide.* London: DCSF.

Beels, P. (2004) 'All about Documentation', *Nursery World,* 5 February, pp. 15–22.

Bilton, H. (2002) *Outdoor Play in the Early Years: Management and Innovation.* London: David Fulton Publishers.

Blatchford, P. (1998) *Social Life in School: Pupils' Experiences of Breaktime and Recess from 7 to 16 Years.* London: Falmer.

British Standards (BSI) (2008) *Playground Equipment and Surfacing: General Safety Requirements and Test Methods.* London: BSI.

Casey, T. (2003) *School Grounds Literature Review.* Edinburgh: Play Scotland/Grounds for Learning/sportscotland.

Casey, T. (2004) *The Play Inclusive Research Report.* Edinburgh: The Yard.

Casey, T. (2007) *Environments for Outdoor Play: A Practical Guide to Making Space for Children.* London: Sage.

Clark, A. (2004) *Why and How we Listen to Young Children.* London: National Children's Bureau.

Cooper, V. and Blake, S. (2004) *Play, Creativity and Emotional and Social Development – Spotlight Briefing.* London: National Children's Bureau.

Council for Disabled Children (2004) *The Dignity of Risk.* London: Council for Disabled Children.

Department for Culture, Media and Sport (DCMS) (2004) *Getting Serious About Play: A Review of Children's Play.* London: DCMS.

Department for Education and Employment (DfEE) (2001) *Building Bulletin 94: Inclusive School Design.* Norwich: The Stationery Office.

Department for Education and Skills (DfES) (2004) *Recruitment and Retention of Disabled People: A Good Practice Guide for Early Years, Childcare and Playwork Providers.* London: DfES and DWP (Department for Work and Pensions).

Department for Children, Schools and Families (DCFS) and Department for Culture, Media and Sport (DCMS) (2008) *Fair Play: A Consultation on the Play Strategy.* London: DCSF and DCMS.

Department for Children, Schools and Families (DCSF) (2008a) *Statutory Framework for the Early Years Foundation Stage.* London: DCSF.

Department for Children, Schools and Families (DCSF) (2008b) *The Play Strategy.* London: DCSF.

Dickens, M. (2004) *Listening to Young Disabled Children.* London: National Children's Bureau.

Douch, P. (2002) *It Doesn't Just Happen: Inclusive Management for Inclusive Play.* London: Kidsactive.

Else, P. (2009) *The Value of Play.* London: Continuum.

European Commission (2009) *Early Childhood Education and Care: Key Lessons from Research for Policy Makers.* Brussels: European Commission.

Equal Opportunities Commission Scotland (undated) *An Equal Start: Promoting Equal Opportunities in the Early Years.* Glasgow: Equal Opportunities Commission Scotland.

Evans, J. (1989) *Children at Play: Life in the School Playground.* Geelong, Victoria, Australia: Deakin University Press.

Gill, T. (2007) *No Fear: Growing Up in a Risk Averse Society.* London: Calouste Gulbenkian Foundation.

Goldschmied, E. and Jackson, S. (2003) *People Under Three: Young Children in Day Care.* London: Routledge.

Gutteridge, S., Legg, J. and Wharton, P. (2007) *Inside Out and Outside In.* Stirling: Stirling Council.

Harrop, P. (2006) *Rope Swings, Dens, Treehouses and Fires: A Risk Based Approach for Managers Facilitating Self-Built Play Structures and Activities in Woodland Settings.* Bristol: Forestry Commission.

Hart, R. (1997) *Children's Participation.* London: Earthscan/UNICEF.

HM Inspectorate of Education (2002) *Count Us In: Achieving Inclusion in Scottish Schools.* Edinburgh: The Stationery Office.

Hodgkin, R. and Newell, P. (2007) *Implementation Handbook for the Convention on the Rights of the Child.* (3rd ed) Geneva: UNICEF.

Hughes, B. (2001) *Evolutionary Playwork and Reflective Analytic Practice.* London: Routledge.

Hughes, B. (2006) *PlayTypes: Speculations and Possibilities.* London: London Centre for Playwork Education and Training.

Humphries, S. and Rowe, S. (1994) 'The Biggest Classroom', in P. Blatchford and S. Sharp (eds) *Breaktime and the School: Understanding and Changing Playground Behaviour.* London: Routledge.

Interboard (2006) *Understanding the Foundation Stage.* Available at: www.nicurriculum. org.uk/docs/foundation_stage/UF_web.pdf

John, A. and Wheway, R. (2004) *Can Play Will Play: Disabled Children and Access to Outdoor Playgrounds.* London: National Playing Fields Association.

Kidsactive (2004a) *Inclusion Checklist for Settings.* London: Kidsactive.

Kidsactive (2004b) *Inclusion Framework for Local Authorities.* London: Kidsactive.

Lancaster, Y.P. (2003) *Promoting Listening to Children: The Reader.* Berkshire: Open University Press.

Lester, S. and Russell, W. (2008) *Play for a Change: Summary Report.* London: Play England.

Louv, R. (2006) *Last Child in the Woods.* New York: Algonquin Books of Chapel Mill.

Maneeterm, L., Chuntawithate, P. and Casey, T. (2001) *Play for Life.* Bangkok: Foundation for Child Development.

Marl, K. (1999) *Accessible Games Book.* London: Jessica Kingsley.

Mayor of London (2004) *Draft Guide to Preparing Play Strategies.* London: Greater London Authority, Children and Young People's Unit.

McIntyre, S. (2007) *People Play Together More: A Handbook for Supporting Inclusive Play.* Edinburgh: The Yard.

Moore, R. (1973) *Open Space Learning Place: School Yards and Other Places as Communal Resources for Environmental Education, Creative Play and Recreation.* San Diego: Department of Landscape Architecture, University of California.

Moss, P. and Petrie, P. (2002) *From Children's Services to Children's Spaces.* London: RoutledgeFalmer.

Murray, D. (2004) *Pick & Mix: A Selection of Inclusive Games and Activities.* London: Kidsactive.

Murray, J. (2002) *Building on Success: Case Studies of Ethos Award Winners 1997–2001.* Edinburgh: Scottish Schools Ethos Network.

National Playing Fields Association (NPFA) (2000) *Best Play: What Play Provision Should do for Children.* London: NPFA/Children's Play Council/PLAYLINK.

Office of the Deputy Prime Minister (ODPM) (2004) *Developing Accessible Play Space: A Good Practice Guide.* London: ODPM.

Office of the First Minister and the Deputy First Minister (OFMDFM) (2009) *The Play and Leisure Policy Statement for Northern Ireland.* Available at: www.allchildrenni.gov.uk/index/play-and-leisure-policy.htm

PLAYLINK (2009) *Risk It! Changing Public Play Spaces.* Conference report. London: PLAYLINK.

Play Safety Forum (2002) *Managing Risk in Play Provision: A Position Statement.* London: Children's Play Council.

Qualifications, Curriculum and Assessment Authority for Wales (2004) *The Foundation Phase in Wales: A Draft Framework for Children's Learning.* Cardiff: ACCAC.

Reiser, R. (2003) *Everybody In. Good Practice in the Identification and Inclusion of Disabled Children and Those with SEN: A Guide for Practitioners and Teachers.* London: Disability Equality in Education.

Rennie, S. (2003) 'Making Play Work: The Fundamental Role of Play in the Development of Social Relationships', in F. Brown (ed.) *Playwork: Theory and Practice.* Buckingham: Open University Press.

Scottish Executive (2001) *Better Behaviour, Better Learning: Summary Report of the Discipline Task Group.* Edinburgh: The Stationery Office.

Scottish Executive (2002) *Guidance on Preparing Accessibility Strategies.* Edinburgh: The Stationery Office.

Scottish Government (2008) *The Early Years Framework Part II.* Edinburgh: Scottish Government.

Shackell, A., Butler, N., Doyle, P. and Ball, D. (2008) *Design for Play: A Guide to Creating Successful Play Spaces.* London: DCMS.

Shephard, C. and Treseder, P. (2002) *Participation: Spice It Up!* Cardiff: Save the Children Fund.

Society for Children and Youth of British Columbia (undated) *Making Space for Children, Rethinking and Re-creating Children's Play Environments.* Vancouver: Society for Children and Youth of British Columbia.

Stirling Council Children's Services (undated) *Inside Out and Outside In.* Stirling: Stirling Council.

Sutcliffe, R. (2008) 'The Play Safety Forum Risk Guide for Play Provision', *International Play Association: PlayRights* 2(8): 14–15.

Sutton-Smith, B. (2001) *The Ambiguity of Play.* Cambridge, MA: Harvard University Press.

Titman, W. (1994) *Special Places, Special People: The Hidden Curriculum of School Grounds.* Godalming: World Wide Fund for Nature/Learning through Landscapes.

UNICEF (1989) Convention on the Rights of the Child. www.unicef.org/crc

United Nations Committee on the Rights of the Child (UNCRC) (2005) *General Comment No.7 Implementing Child Rights in Early Childhood.* Available at: www2.ohchr.org/english/bodies/CRC/comments.htm

United Nations Committee on the Rights of the Child (UNCRC) (2006) *General Comment No. 9: The Rights of Disabled Children.* Available at: www2.ohchr.org/english/ bodies/CRC/comments.htm

United Nations Committee on the Rights of the Child (UNCRC) (2008*) Concluding Observations: United Kingdom of Great Britain and Northern Ireland.* Available at: www2. ohchr.org/english/bodies/CRC/docs/AdvanceVersions/CRC.C.GBR.CO.4.pdf

van Gils, J. (2008) *The UN Convention on the Rights of the Child and the Evolution of Children's Play.* Speech to International Council on Children's Play conference, Bruno.

Welsh Assembly Government (WAG) (2006) *Play in Wales: The Assembly Government's Play Policy Implementation Plan,* Cardiff: Welsh Assembly Government.

Welsh Assembly Government (WAG) (2006) *The Play Policy.* Cardiff: Welsh Assembly Government.

Widdowson, J.D.A. (2001) 'Rhythm, Repetition and Rhetoric: Learning Language in the School Playground', in J.C. Bishop and M. Curtis (eds) *Play Today in the Primary School Playground.* Philadelphia, PA: Open University Press.

Yearley, D. (2007) *Play and the Natural Environment.* Keynote speech given at ROSPA Conference, June 14, 2007 Loughborough.

Index

Exciting Early Years and Primary Texts from SAGE

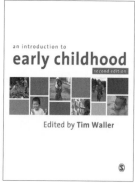

an introduction to
early childhood
second edition

Edited by **Tim Waller**

978-1-84787-518-1

Development & Learning
for **Very Young Children**
Hilary Fabian & Claire Mould

978-1-84787-393-4

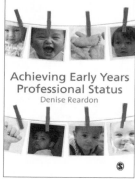

**Achieving Early Years
Professional Status**
Denise Reardon

978-1-84787-190-9

Research Methods in
Early Childhood
An Introductory Guide
Penny Mukherji and Deborah Albon

978-1-84787-524-2

The Early Years Foundation Stage
Theory and Practice

Edited by Ioanna Palaiologou

978-1-84860-127-7

5th EDITION

**CONTEMPORARY
ISSUES IN THE
EARLY YEARS**

edited by
GILLIAN PUGH
BERNADETTE DUFFY

978-1-84787-593-8

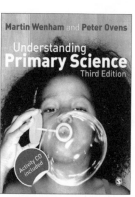

Martin Wenham and Peter Ovens
Understanding
Primary Science
Third Edition

Activity CD included

978-1-84860-119-2

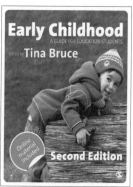

Early Childhood
A GUIDE FOR EDUCATION STUDENTS
Edited by **Tina Bruce**

Online material included

Second Edition

978-1-84860-224-3

**Mathematics
Explained** for
primary teachers
4th edition
Derek Haylock

Online material included

978-1-84860-197-0

Find out more about these titles and our wide range of books for education students and practitioners at **www.sagepub.co.uk/education**

Exciting Education Texts from SAGE

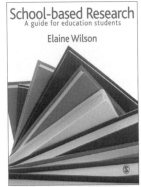

School-based Research
A guide for education students
Elaine Wilson

978-1-4129-4850-0

TEACHING **ENGLISH**

DEVELOPING AS A REFLECTIVE SECONDARY TEACHER

CAROL EVANS
ALYSON MIDGLEY
PHIL RIGBY
LYNNE WARHAM
PETER WOOLNOUGH

978-1-4129-4818-0

Achieving your
PTLLS Award
A Practical Guide to Successful Teaching in the Lifelong Learning Sector

Mary Francis
Jim Gould

978-1-84787-917-2

Introduction to
**Research
Methods** in
Education

Keith F
Punch

978-1-84787-018-6

A Toolkit
for the effective
Teaching
Assistant

2nd Edition

Maureen Parker, Chris Lee, Stuart Gunn,
Kitty Heardman, Rachael Hincks,
Mary Pittman and Mark Townsend

978-1-84787-943-1

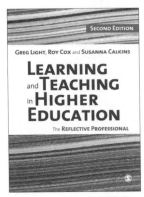

SECOND EDITION

GREG LIGHT, ROY COX and SUSANNA CALKINS

LEARNING
and **TEACHING**
in **HIGHER
EDUCATION**
The **REFLECTIVE PROFESSIONAL**

978-1-84860-008-9

TEACHING **SCIENCE**

DEVELOPING AS A REFLECTIVE SECONDARY TEACHER

TONY LIVERSIDGE
MATT COCHRANE
BERNARD KERFOOT
JUDITH THOMAS

978-1-84787-362-0

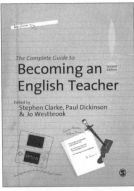

The Complete Guide to
Becoming an Second Edition
English Teacher

Edited by
Stephen Clarke, Paul Dickinson
& Jo Westbrook

978-1-84787-289-0

3rd Edition

Daniel Muijs and David Reynolds
Effective Teaching
Evidence and Practice

978-1-84920-076-9

Find out more about these titles and our wide range of books for
education students and practitioners at **www.sagepub.co.uk/education**